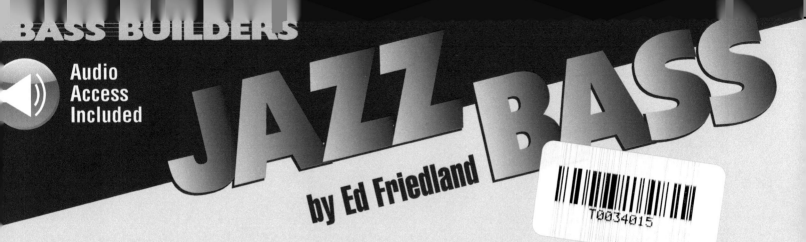

BASS BUILDERS

Audio Access Included

JAZZ BASS

by Ed Friedland

T0034015

To access audio visit:
www.halleonard.com/mylibrary

6065-6367-1389-0515

Cover photos courtesy of CARVIN.

ISBN 978-0-7935-6517-7

HAL•LEONARD®
CORPORATION

7777 W. BLUEMOUND RD. P.O. BOX 13819 MILWAUKEE, WI 53213

Visit Hal Leonard on the internet at http://www.halleonard.com

Table of Contents

Part One

Part Two

Preface

Many different skills are required to become a functional bass player in the jazz idiom. First there is profiency with the instrument. Then there is understanding the role of the bass in jazz. A combination of theoretical knowledge and finely tuned ears are also necessary. Familiarity with the stylistic nuances of the many types of jazz is another requirement. Finally, you must know the standard performance format that jazz musicians use, and its many variations, have a keen memory for tunes, and common sense "street wisdom." If you have all these skills under your belt, you will be as prepared as anyone can be to go out into the jazz world and function competently. Many of these skills must be acquired and honed over a period of time. The time-honored tradition of trial and error is an important part of the jazz learning experience. You have all the information in the world and years of practicing at home behind you, but the essential moment when you step out and play, putting yourself on the line, that is when school begins.

Goal Statement

This book will attempt to provide you with practical information about the essential skills of playing jazz bass. It will not substitute for the years of experience needed to become a professional jazz musician, but it will answer some questions that you might feel foolish asking on your first gig. It is a well known fact that jazz musicians place a certain value on being perceived as "hip" (myself included). Being hip at its most basic, is knowing what is going on. It is my intention to "hip" you to as much useful information about jazz playing as possible. For example, we will learn to keep track of song form, construct functional walking bass lines, play in 3/4, Latin, and ballad feels. We will learn the numerical shorthand system that helps musicians communicate quickly, take a brief look at soloing, examine some of the most common intros and endings, learn standard performance protocol, and then put all of this knowledge into action.

There will be opportunities to play along with a band on the audio. These tracks will simulate actual playing conditions. Unfortunately, due to the nature of recorded music, once you've heard it, it will no longer hold the element of surprise. The surprise factor is a large part of the jazz experience: you have to be open to whatever happens. Jazz, in its truest form, is a living thing. It breathes, flows; it can change directions like the wind. The same tune will never be played exactly the same way twice. This living element will only be experienced when you get out there and play with other people. Therefore, the better prepared you are for your jazz experience, the more you (and those you play with) will enjoy it.

From my experiences playing jazz in Boston and New York City, I have learned many useful lessons about what it takes to survive and thrive in the jazz environment. I gladly share these lessons with you, with the hope that they will inspire you to venture into the world of jazz.

Acknowledgments

Thanks to Sonia, Lee Ellen and Aimee Friedland, David Taylor, Jeff Haskell, Fred Hayes, Tom Ervin, Greg Armstrong, Jim Brady, Larry and Pam Fishman and Fishman Tranducers, Peter Tillotson, John Styklunas, the staff at Hal Leonard Corporation, Bill Brinkley, Dave Flores and everyone at Carvin, LaBella Strings, Athena, and TBL. Thanks to all my teachers, in their many forms. And thanks to all the great drummers in the world who make playing bass fun.

About the Author

Ed Friedland is a graduate of the High School of Music and Art in New York City, and a former member of the Bass Department at Berklee College of Music in Boston. He is a frequent contributor to *Bass Player Magazine*, and is the author of *Building Walking Bass Lines* and *Expanding Walking Bass Lines*, also available from the Hal Leonard Corporation. His performance credits include Larry Coryell, Michal Urbaniak, Robben Ford, Mike Metheny, Sal Nistico, Illinois Jaquette, Johnny Adams, Linda Hopkins, Robert Junior Lockwood, Barrence Whitfield and the Savages, Martha and the Vandellas, The Drifters, The Marvelletes, Brook Benton, the Boston and Tokyo productions of *Little Shop of Horrors*, the Opera company of Boston, and the Boston production of *A Closer Walk with Patsy Cline*. Ed is involved in producing and arranging with Bass Station Music. He has a M.Ed. from Cambridge College, Cambridge, Massachusetts. He uses Carvin basses, LaBella strings and Fishman Transducers. Ed resides in Tucson, Arizona.

Using the Audio

The audio portion is crucial to the effectiveness of this method. The nature of playing the bass is to be an accompanist. Most of what we play is within the context of a group of musicians. It could be a duo, or it could be a 17-piece big band, but there are always others involved. To grasp the skills you need to function as a bassist, you must learn to use them in context. For the bassist learning at home, I have provided a variety of pre-recorded examples to use with the contents of this book. As I have said, while these tracks will not substitute for playing with live musicians, they will be a useful tool for your development.

The audio uses a split-stereo mix with piano and drums on the right channel, and bass and drums on the left channel. All horns will be placed on the right with the piano. This configuration will allow you to turn off the bass track and play with the other instruments. It will also allow you to study the bass tracks closely, and even transcribe them. You can use the Playback+ function to hear the tracks online.

The examples in the book marked with an audio 🔊 icon have a number that corresponds to the number on the audio. The example number is given and then counted off with a two bar click. Some examples will have a regular count off that is typical of a jazz performance. Instead of a click, you will hear me speak the count off, and my fingers snap on beats two and four. This is the way tunes are counted off on the gig.

The Glossary

You may not be familiar with all the terms commonly used to describe musical events. Jazz in particular has its own set of terms. When you are confronted with a new term, look in the glossary at the back of the book, you should find it there.

Part One

The first skill you need to become a successful bassist in any style is the ability to keep time. Those of you familiar with my books *Building Walking Bass Lines* and *Expanding Walking Bass Lines*, or have seen my articles in *Bass Player Magazine* "The Metronome as Guru" (*BP* 4/93) and "Grooving on the Grid" (*BP* 8/95) will already know that I am a tireless advocate of time keeping. Let's face facts, everyone that hires a bass player wants them to keep time. No one has ever been fired from a gig because their time was too good. I suggest that you regularly use a metronome to develop your sense of time. Some people claim that using the metronome will make you sound mechanical and stiff. I must disagree. You are human, subject to a wide range of human inconsistencies. When you play with other humans, this factor is multiplied, thus creating a living, breathing feel. Using a metronome to strengthen your time feel will not turn you into a time zombie. What it will do is develop your internal clock so you can be the grounding force in music that a bass player needs to be.

Drummers

In addition to developing the ability to keep a consistent pulse, you must learn to lock in with the drummer. On gigs without drummers, the bassist becomes even more responsible for the time. With a drummer, you need to find the common ground upon which to tread. Drummers are equally responsible for the time; it is the rhythm section that keeps the band grooving. We would like to assume that all drummers take this responsibility as seriously as we hope all bass players do. Unfortunately, there is too often a lack of attention to this issue on both sides of the fence. The rhythm section's first priority needs to be keeping time. If all the bass player cares about is the bass solo, the groove won't happen. Similarly, if all the drummer cares about is using his new Tony Williams lick every sixteen measures, it won't happen. Enter into the rhythm section with the spirit of cooperation. No single person will sound good without the help of the other. Often, this means making subtle adjustments in approach. Different drummers approach playing time in their own unique way. Sometimes they have the ability to adjust to you, or to the band as a whole. But often, it is up to you to make the adjustments. Rather than try to dictate the flow, go with it. This, of course, assumes there are no major problems with the time. If a drummer is slowing down, then you'll have to give him a big kick in the pants. If he is speeding up, then you have to dig in and keep your foot on the brakes. Unfortunately, these situations will happen more often than you would like. This reality makes an even stronger case for bassists to focus on time keeping. Therefore, the stronger you are with the time, the greater your chances are for creating a positive force in less than ideal situations.

Not all rhythm sections have these problems. The best possible scenario is two great musicians, one a drummer, the other a bassist getting together and creating a groove so strong that it can lift the entire band to unimaginable heights of creativity. Fortunately, this happens, but not without cooperation. The saddest thing is when you have two great musicians, but one or both refuses to let go of where *they* think the groove should be. This happens way too often. When you start to play with a drummer, you need to quickly assess the situation. Does he play with an edge, on top of the beat? Is he laid back, playing slightly behind? Maybe he is right smack in the middle. Does the drummer play like anyone you've ever heard on a record? (Of course he does!) Try to identify the influences you're hearing and play accordingly. There are many great rhythm pairs in the history of recorded jazz. Listen to them. Learn to adapt your playing to the style that is currently being played on your gig. While some may feel it is best to develop your own conception and be uncompromising to your ideals, I suggest that you learn as many different styles as possible, and learn to create something uniquely yours. You must have the flexibility to adjust because, most likely, no one else will. And, yes, there are times when you just play with a drummer and everything clicks. There is no struggle to keep time; you play freely without concern for the groove because you *know* it's there. These are the best experiences in the world. You find yourself energized by the music, you play things you never knew you could, and you enter the trance-like state of groove bliss. Savor it, for there is nothing finer in the whole world.

The Big Couch

No, this does not have anything to do with psychotherapy. While we are discussing time, I'd like to bring up the concept of playing the different areas of the beat. This is commonly referred to as playing behind the beat, ahead of the beat, or in the middle of the beat. While you can't necessarily notate this phenomenon, it can be felt. It is possible to play in each of these three areas of the beat without speeding up or slowing down. The key is to be centered. This can be achieved by working out with the metronome in a consistent and focused manner. Another tool to understanding this is a visualization I call "The Big Couch." Imagine you have a couch that is six feet long. Now imagine that this couch is balanced like a see-saw. If we were to try to get comfortable we would need to sit in the middle. So we align our god-given center line right at the three foot mark. Now we can sit back and relax. Let's say we want to lean over to the left to get some potato chips, no problem. Maybe we need to get the remote control, it's on the right, so we lean over and pick it up. Okay, this works fine as long as we are aligned with the center. Now imagine that we move over one inch to the right. Suddenly, the couch isn't so comfortable anymore. We have to compensate to the left to stay level. Leaning over to the left is harder due to the extra reach needed. Leaning over to the right becomes very dangerous because we're already seated to the right. Toppling over is very possible. What if we were sitting two inches to the right? Forget about the remote control, all our energy goes into just trying to stay level. The couch is no longer a comfortable place.

This is an obvious metaphor for playing the different areas of the beat. If we are centered, then we can play on top of the beat comfortably without speeding up, and behind the beat without slowing down. Sometimes we need to use this centering to help counter the effect of another player that is sitting too far to the left or right. To hear some good examples of this concept in action, I recommend you listen to the following rhythm sections.

- Eddie Gomez and Steve Gadd, on Chick Corea's *Three Quartets* are a great example of playing on top of the beat.

- Sam Jones and Billy Higgins, on Cedar Walton's *Eastern Rebellion* are a terrific example of behind the beat grooving.

- Paul Chambers and Jimmy Cobb, on the classic Miles Davis album *Kind of Blue* are swinging hard, right down the center.

There are many other great recorded examples of these three areas of the beat. As you listen to jazz, determine where the rhythm section is laying: on top, behind, or in the middle. After a while, you'll have the sound and feel firmly in your head. As you develop a centered time feel, you will be able to play in any area you want, thus making you a flexible and undoubtedly in-demand bassist.

Rhythmic Development

Now that we have explored the nature of time, let's do some work. This series of rhythmic drills is an excerpt from an article I wrote for *Bass Player Magazine*, "Grooving on the Grid" (*BP* 8/95). The idea behind these exercises is to develop an internal understanding of these rhythms. Rhythm exists in time, and a bar of 4/4 has a finite amount of space to be filled. While it has been known to be stretched beyond these limits (usually when trading fours with the drums), we would like to deal with a bar of 4/4 as a finite entity. If we accept this, then the division of a bar of 4/4 into smaller units must occur in an accurate way. We will use the metronome to help us develop accuracy, but the nature of these examples will insure that you will not become mechanical.

To play rhythms accurately and with feeling you need to know them from the inside out. You have to let the rhythm become part of your body. The most direct route to this type of understanding is to vocalize. There is an old saying in jazz: "If you can't sing it, you can't play it." This is especially true of rhythm. Singing rhythms will help you develop an internal understanding. Indian classical music has been taught this way for centuries. Before tabla drum students are allowed to actually play the drum, they must first learn to sing the language of the rhythms used in Indian music. A complex system of syllables that correspond to every sound on the drum is taught. When the student is finally allowed to play the drum, all that need be learned are the mechanics of the instrument, and the marriage of technique and rhythmic language. This method insures that the rhythm will come from inside the musician.

Each of the following examples has syllables that correspond to rhythmic content. The first step is to learn the syllables. The syllables contained in parenthesis are sung but not played. They are there to fill up the rests that occurs between the rhythms. These rests must also be accurate. You have to groove during the rests as well. Eventually, you may not feel the need to sing the rests, but it is important at first because it helps you keep track of where you are in the measure.

This first group of rhythms is based on the eighth-note triplet. The triplet is the underlying pulse in Swing-oriented jazz. Triplets have a round, wave-like quality that can be stretched and pulled. For our purposes, we want them to lay evenly, right down the middle. Practice each example separately in a loop. Then connect them into an eight measure example.

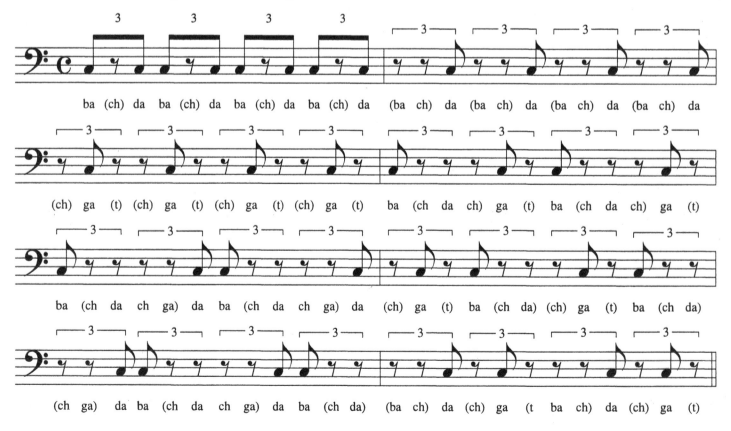

The next set of rhythms are sixteenth-note based. They are a common subdivision in Latin, rock, "ECM" and fusion styles of jazz. Sixteenth-note groupings can be seen as little square boxes that move up and down. As with the triplet examples, some of these will contain syllables that are sung but not played. Again, practice each one individually, then string them together for an eight measure loop.

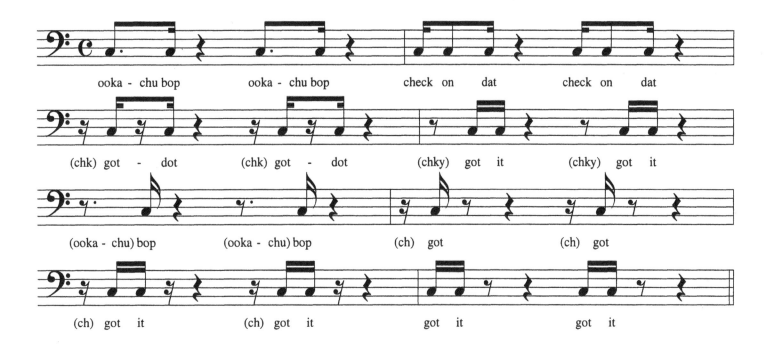

These exercises will strengthen your groove on sixteenth-note and eighth-note triplet feels. They will also develop your ability to read rhythms. Giving each rhythm a set of syllables creates a "memory tag" that will help you identify them on sight. Rather than panic when handed a piece that contains many sixteenth-note rhythms, you will see your old friends "ooka chu bop" and "check on dat." Trust me, this really does work.

Chord Construction

To play jazz, one must thoroughly know all the chord structures commonly found in the music. When walking or soloing, we use the information contained in the chord symbol to determine what notes are available to us. Here is a list of common chord types.

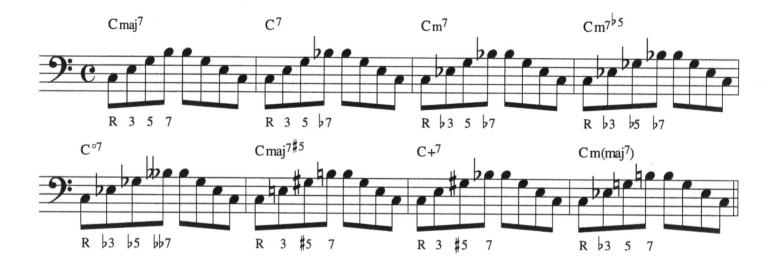

The Numerical Shorthand System

The Numerical Shorthand System is a very useful tool for understanding jazz and all other types of music. Basically, we take the major scale (do, re, me, fa, sol, la, ti, do) and assign numbers to each note. One through eight is do to do. The major scale is the reference point for melodic and harmonic structure.

The scale is shown with both Arabic and Roman numerals. These numbers refer to specific notes that occur in melodies, within chord structures, or to chord structures that make up a progression. Each note in the scale has a corresponding chord structure built up from it. By using only the notes contained in the scale for these structures, we arrive at a set of chords that reflect the tonality of the key center. These are called diatonic chord structures.

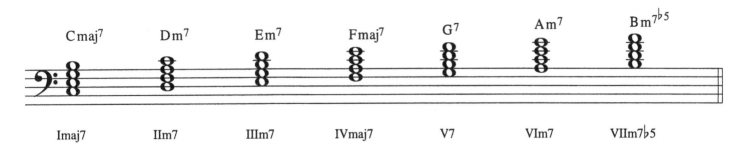

Tunes are sequences of chords that exist in a key. Most tunes will have more than one key center within its form, but will always revolve to one particular key center. If a tune is said to be in the key of B♭, then all the numbers are applied to the notes from B♭. As well, all chords in the tune are related to the numbers as they occur in the key of B♭.

For example, this would be I-VI-II-V in the key of B♭.

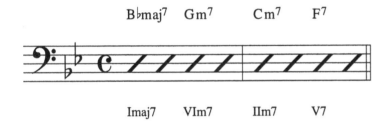

Using this system, it is possible to communicate an entire song very quickly. For example, a pianist might describe a tune by saying "It's I-VI-II-V-III-VI-II-V, II-V of IV to IV minor, then III-VI-II-V. That repeats, the second ending resolves to the I, and then goes to the bridge, which is III7, VI7, II7, V7, two bars each. Then go back to the I-VI-II-V for the last A." Got it? As confusing as this may sound at first, once you understand the numerical shorthand system, it becomes a very effective way of learning tunes.

Here is the tune that the piano player described, written out in full form. Look it over and see if you can combine the description with the actual song.

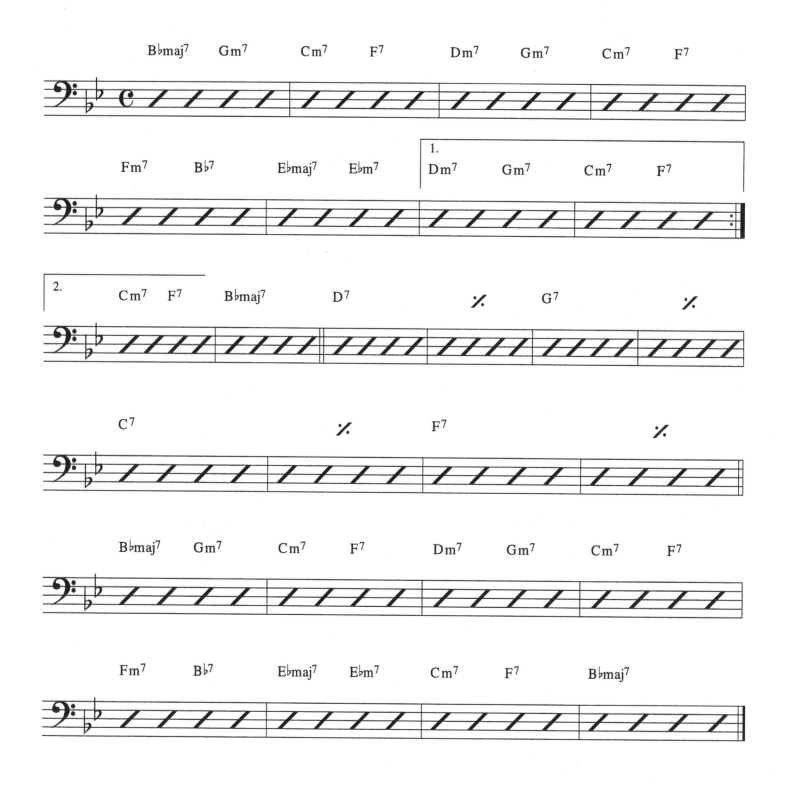

This system also gives you a generic map of a tune you can use to transpose the tune to another key. If you understand the relationships between the root motions you can learn a song in any key. These relationships are represented by the intervals between the roots. The distance between Imaj7 and VIm7 is the same in any key. These distances are also represented by physical shapes on the fingerboard. The shape for the root motion of I to VI is the same in any key (with the exceptions created by using open strings).

Transposing songs to different keys is an important skill for the jazz bassist, particularly when playing with singers. Since a large percentage of jazz gigs involve backing up a singer, you need to learn to transpose. Jazz singers mostly do songs out of the standard repertoire, but often in different keys. If you can play a tune in B♭, you should be able to play it in all the other keys as well.

Here are a few short progressions written out in numeric shorthand. They will appear on the audio in three different keys, first in the key of F, then the key of A♭, and last in the key of E♭. For now, you don't have to walk through the changes, you can simply play the roots in each key. Later on you will have the opportunity to transpose an entire tune from a set of changes in the original key. Before we start to play with the band, we need to get in tune. Here is tuning note G.

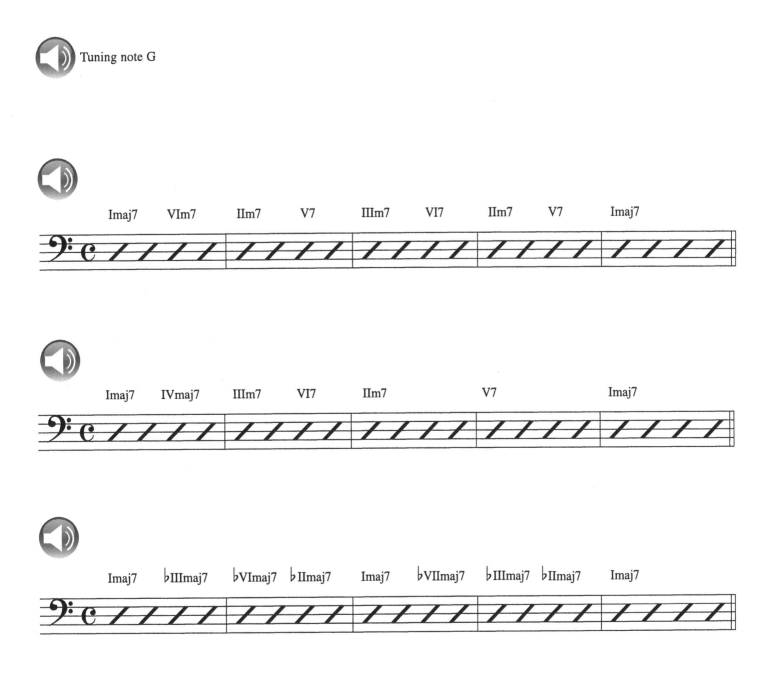

Keeping the Form

The form is the length and structure of a song. Keeping track of the framework of a tune is of monumental importance. When you lose the form, you have essentially thrown a big wrench into the works. This *will* happen to you (if it hasn't already). It is a rite of passage for all bass players. At first you will get lost often, then, as you play tunes over and over, you'll learn the form and keep your place. Although losing the form is a big problem, it is repairable. It is possible to get back to the right place if you do four things.

First, *relax*. If you panic about being lost, it will be much harder to find your way back. Second, *listen*. There are many cues being played that will help you find your way. Drum fills most often happen at the end of four or eight measure phrases, bigger ones lead in or out of the bridge and drummers usually do something distinctive to mark the top of the next chorus. Third, *keep your eyes open*. Often players will close their eyes while they get deep into the trance of jazz. This is fine, except if you become lost in the form (or should be looking for a visual cue from someone). Once you realize you're lost, open your eyes and look around at the people you are playing with (try not to look too terrified). Usually someone is willing to be helpful for the sake of keeping the tune from becoming a train wreck. You can look to that sympathetic soul for a cue. Unfortunately, in the big-city approach to learning jazz, many players will take the attitude of "sink or swim." If the form gets mixed up, they'll glare at you like a vegetarian at a cattle rancher's convention. Don't look for any help from them. Some people will actually ignore your need for help, sacrificing the tune, just to teach you a lesson. And you will learn it, believe me. There's nothing like making a fool of yourself, especially in front of a lot of people, to instill a desire to improve a skill. Fourth, *don't stop playing!* If we prioritize a bassist's primary obligations, the first is to keep the pulse, the second is to keep the form, and the third is to create bass lines that contain harmonic and rhythmic material relevant to the piece being played. With this hierarchy in mind, if you've lost the form, numbers two and three are no longer possible, but number one still has a chance if you keep plowing through. So, keep playing strong, even if the notes are all wrong. It's better to be at least thirty-three percent right instead of being one hundred percent wrong, which is what you'll be if you stop playing altogether.

Eventually, you'll figure out ways to manage being lost without anyone even knowing. It is possible to be vague, even oblique in your reference to the harmony so you can play through being lost. That is you are neither right nor wrong, you're just there. This is preferable to not being there. In the midst of this charade, you are using all the above mentioned tactics to find your way home. It's not an ideal situation, but as you venture out into the world of playing jazz, you will undoubtedly find yourself there. Hopefully, forearmed with this information, you won't have to visit too often or stay too long.

The best suggestion I can make about learning to keep your place in a song is to learn the melody. If you learn to hear the melody of a song, you can always keep track of the form, even during a drum solo. Since it is not possible to include melodies in this book, you will have to take this step on your own. Listen to recordings of tunes you play, and learn to sing along with the melody. If you learn a song out of a "fake book" you can learn the melody by reading it.

Common Forms

Now let's look at some of the more common forms you will encounter in jazz playing. The first form is the twelve-bar blues. This form is common not only in jazz, but in blues (obviously), r&b, country, rock 'n' roll, and funk. Virtually all styles of music have tunes based on the blues form. In addition to having twelve bars, blues forms also have a fairly set harmonic structure. They use mostly dominant seventh chords, and they generally conform to a particular harmonic placement. The blues starts on the I7 chord, sometimes going to the IV7 in the second bar, but not always. In measure four we will sometimes see the IIm7-V7 of the IV chord lead into measure five. The IV7 chord will definitely show up in bar five, then go back to the I7 or some related chord (usually IIImin7) in measure 7. Bar nine brings on the V7 chord, but most often it is preceded by its partner in crime the IImin7, delaying the V7 until bar ten. Bar eleven will be divided by the I7 or IIImin7, or possibly III7, on the first two beats, going to VI7 on beat three. Bar twelve is the IImin7 going to V7. The last two bars of the blues form make up what we call a turn around, a short harmonic pattern that sets up a return to the top of the form. The turn around is an important guide post in the form. It is usually obvious to the ear, and it is commonly known to be the last two bars of the tune. Here is a visual breakdown of the twelve-bar blues.

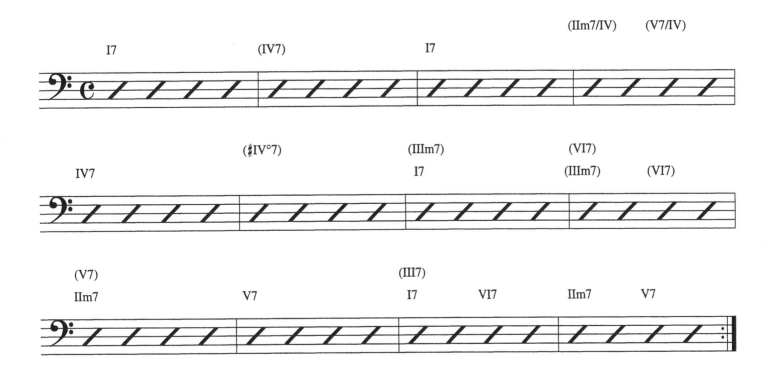

The most common structure is the thirty-two measure AABA form. Countless standards and jazz tunes are based on this form. While the actual harmony of these tunes will differ, the form itself has some distinguishing features that can be identified. All the sections of the form are eight measures in length. The first A section will have a turnaround in the last one or two bars that leads back to the second A. The A section will then repeat, either resolving to the tonic of the piece in measure fifteen (often followed by a turnaround to the bridge), or substituting measures fifteen and/or sixteen with a turn around to the bridge. The bridge will be eight measures long, and may possibly be in a different key from the rest of the tune. The end of the bridge will turn around to the beginning of the last A section. The last A is usually the same as the second A, resolving to the tonic in the last two measures of the form. There is usually a turn around back to the top of the form. Even if a turn around isn't written on the chart, most bass players will add one as a matter of course. The AABA form can be written out in two different ways. The first way we will look at is the long form where each section is written out completely, without the use of repeat signs.

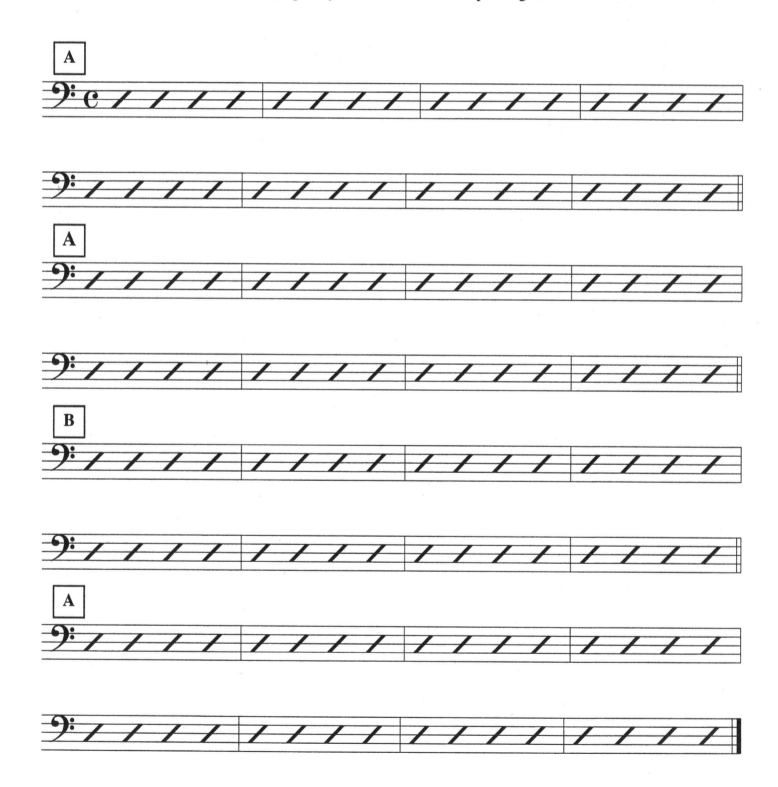

This is the short way to write out the AABA form. Instead of writing out each section in full, a repeat sign is placed at the end of the first A. This leads back to the top of the form. Measures seven and/or eight will be the first ending. This is indicated with a bracket over the measures, often containing a small number one. After taking the repeat, skip the measures contained within the first ending bracket and go to the second ending. This will lead into the bridge. After the bridge, two things are possible: either the last A section is written out fully, or a D.S. (Dal Segno) sign is placed at the end of the bridge, indicating a return to the top of the form. A skip to the second ending is the end of the form, indicated by *al fine* (to the *fine*). This last practice saves time when writing out a chart, but is slightly confusing visually. Here is the short form AABA written in both variations.

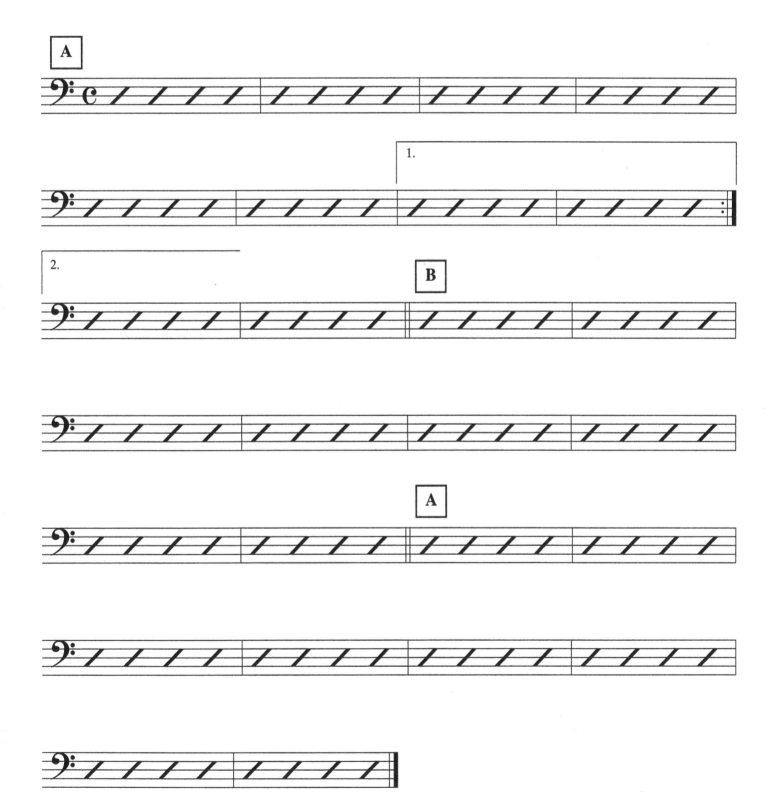

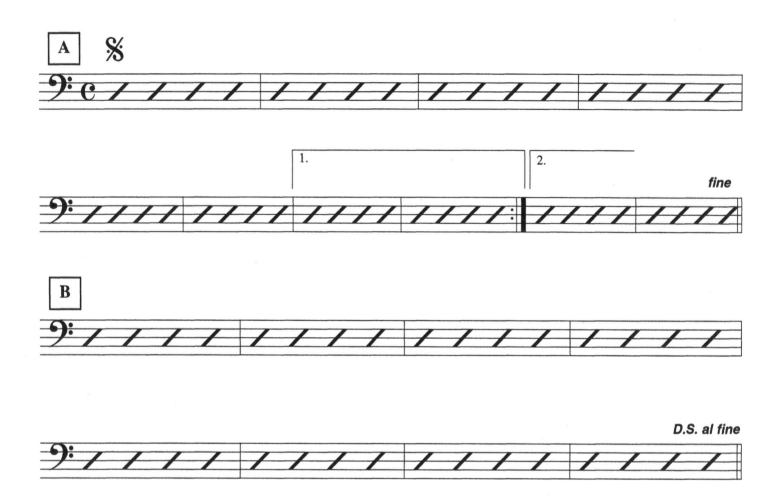

The next form we will examine is the thirty-two measure ABAC form. The A section is an eight measure phrase that leads into the B section. The B section is also eight measures and leads back to the A section. The second A section leads to the C section (also eight measures), which is often similar to the B section, but perhaps with a different ending. Sometimes the C section will have altogether different material from the B, but in every case, it will resolve in the last two measures to the tonic-key center of the tune.

In general, it is true that tunes resolve to the tonic in the last two measures. If you have a question as to the key of a song, look at the last two measures and you will see the answer. The only catch that may arise is when a song resolves to its relative major or minor key. For example, a song in B♭ major may resolve to a G minor seventh chord, or in reverse, a song in the key of G minor may end on a B♭ major seventh chord.

The ABAC form is most often written straight through without repeats, though it may appear in a first ending/second ending configuration, particularly if it is hand written right before the gig. Here is the ABAC form written out both ways.

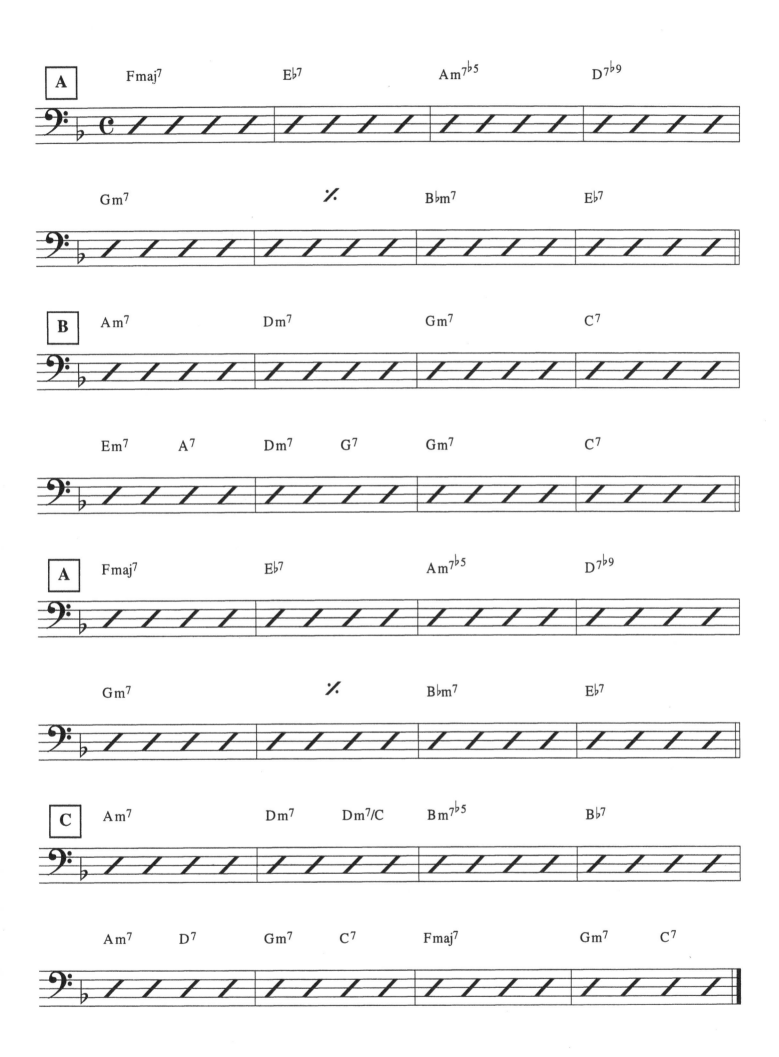

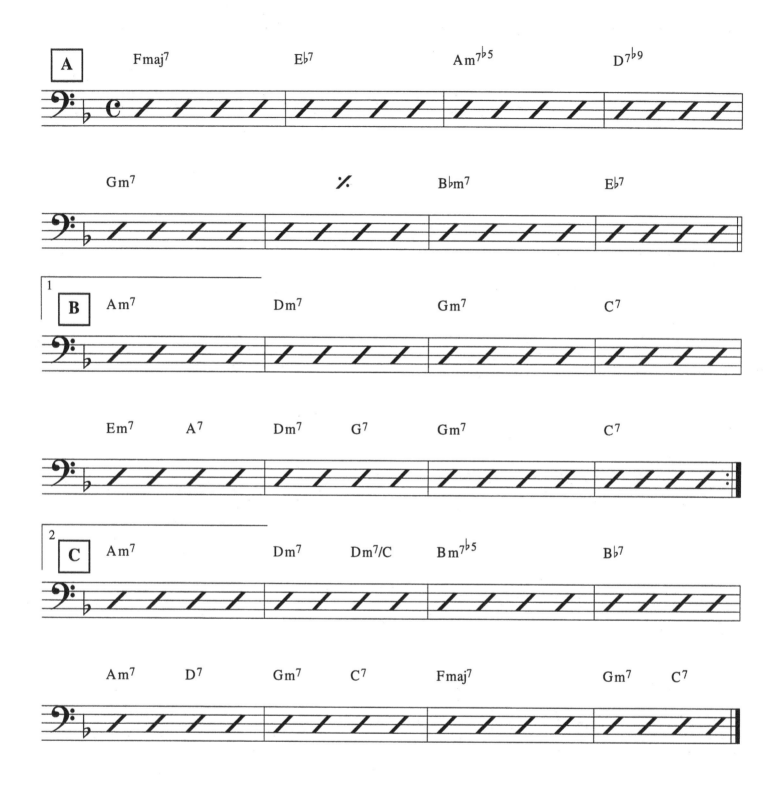

There are certainly other types of forms used in jazz tunes, however these three are the most common. Sometimes a variation of the standard form is used. For example, it is not unusual to have a four-measure extension (called a tag) on the last A section of an AABA or ABAC form. Cole Porter wrote many songs using standard forms, but double in length. A sixteen-measure A section repeats, to a sixteen-measure B section, and back to a sixteen-measure A. Another extended form he wrote with was ABABCCDAB ("Cheek To Cheek"), each section being eight measures long! Needless to say, this song feels like it will never end, and until you learn the song, it takes a lot of concentration to keep your place.

Walking

Walking a bass line is the most typical approach a bass player takes to playing jazz. While other types of rhythmic activity are available, in swing-oriented jazz, we play quarter notes most of the time. The material presented here is a condensation of my book *Building Walking Bass Lines*. You can get the basic idea from what is shown here, but for a more in-depth understanding, I recommend working through that book and its follow up, *Expanding Walking Bass Lines*.

Start with the Roots

The primary objective of a walking line is to outline the chord structure of the song and keep the rhythmic flow of the performance moving. Our note choices must contain pertinent information about the harmonic structure of the tune. We will first use the "target/approach" technique to build our bass lines. By choosing a target note, our lines will have a feeling of destination. We will then use approach notes to precede the target note in order to create a sense of movement.

The first order of business is the root motion. Playing the root of each new chord is the first step toward developing a bass line. Here is an example of using the root motion of a progression to create a walking line.

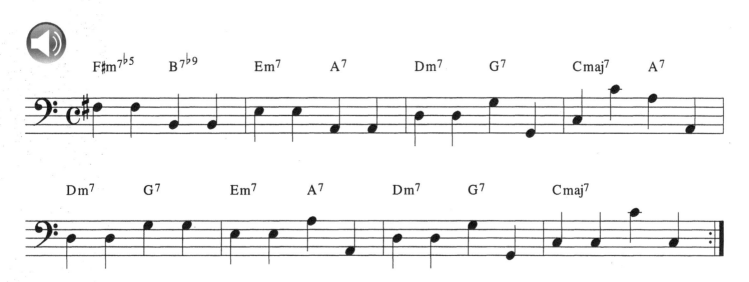

As a jazz bassist, you will rarely have to read written walking lines. The idea is to make up your own from a chord chart or lead sheet. Now practice finding the roots of this progression.

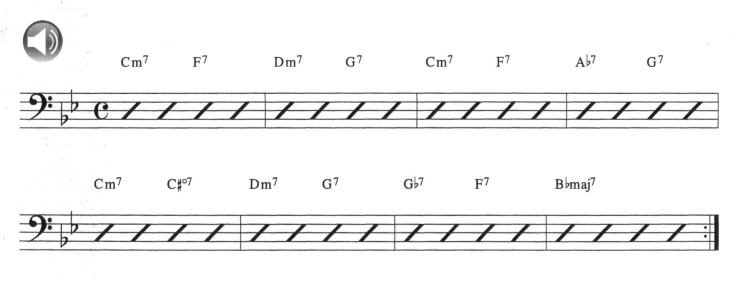

21

Adding the Fifth

The next note we will target is the fifth. To locate the fifth, start on the root and count up the major scale to the fifth note. The fifth is an important structural element of any chord type. The root, fifth, and octave of a chord, are the infrastructure, while the thirds and sevenths create the characteristic quality of a chord. Because all chords have a root, fifth, and octave, they are good all purpose notes to have at your beck and call. They will enable you to at least function in a song until you learn more about the specifics, such as which chords are major or minor, and which chords have major sevenths or minor sevenths.

Here is an example of using roots and fifths to create a walking line through a blues progression.

Now practice playing roots and fifths through this short turn-around progression. Look for several different ways to play this. Use different octaves and different fingerboard locations for the same note to find your options.

Approach Notes

With the root and fifth as our primary targets, we will now add approach notes to give movement to the line. Approach notes precede their target note and create a resolution pattern. This draws on the classic "tension/release" phenomenon that is a significant aspect of all types of music. The approach note creates tension that is released into the target note. An important concept to keep in mind when creating bass lines is gravity. Bass players work with the gravitational pull of the approach/target relationship. Each type of approach discussed has its own type of gravity. Pay attention to how these approaches feel when they connect with their intended target.

Chromatic Approach

The first approach method we will use is the chromatic approach. A chromatic approach is one-half step above or below the target. In this example, we will use upper and lower chromatic approach notes to target the roots and fifths of the chord progression. Roots will be marked with an "R," fifths with a "5," and chromatic approaches with "chr."

Now practice using the chromatic approach on this short turn-around progression. Again, look for as many options as you can.

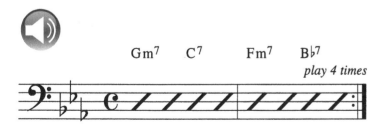

23

Scale Approach

A scale approach resolves to a target note from its upper or lower adjacent scale tone. Usually, this means a whole step above or below the target. In some cases, the scale approach might be a half step away, technically making it a chromatic approach. It doesn't really matter what you call it, just as long as you are within the right scale. For example, let's say you are on a Cmaj7 and the next chord is Fmaj7. The lower scale approach note would be E. This is also chromatic. If you chose E♭, it would be a whole step, but it wouldn't fit the scale since there is no E♭ in the scale that connects these two chords (the C major scale). The scale approach is marked "sc." The approach on beat four of measure one is both scale and chromatic, so it is marked "sc/chr." There are several other approaches that are also the fifth of the chord. Due to their placement directly in front of a target note, they function primarily as approach notes, but they are chord tones as well. These are marked "sc/5."

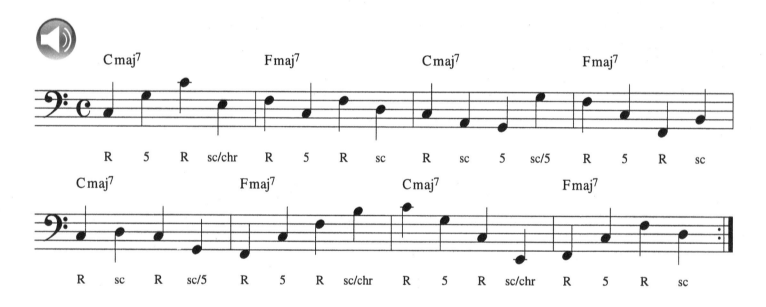

In the previous example, notice that scale approach from below the fifth of each chord was not used. Because these are major chords, the lower scale approach to the fifth (scale-degree four) creates a half step conflict with the major third contained in the chord. It is best to avoid this, for now.

Now it's your turn to figure out some possibilities using the scale approach. As before, the turn-around will repeat four times. Use this opportunity to find as many different ways through this progression as you can.

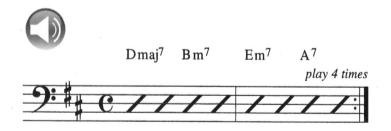

Dominant Approach

The last approach method we will look at is dominant approach. Dominant approach precedes the target with its fifth (called the "dominant") from above or below. It's important to realize that from either above or below the dominant approach is the same note, just in a different octave. The dominant resolution that occurs (also called a "five-one resolution") carries a lot of weight. The five resolving to one is a very strong pattern. Many chord progressions are built with the "five-one" resolution. We call this "dominant root motion" or we say the progression follows the "circle of fifths."

This example uses dominant approach.

In the previous example, you can see there are many notes that are both a dominant approach and a chord tone. When the chord progression follows the dominant pattern, the roots and fifths themselves become approaches. These progressions are very common in all forms of popular music. The strong resolution pattern of the root motion makes for a very compelling progression.

Now that we have looked at the common approaches to our root, fifth, and octave target notes, let's put them all together. This line uses everything we've discussed up to this point. Learn to play it, and analyze it to see how all the approaches are being used.

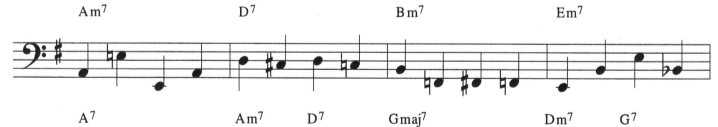

Now it's time to play your own line. Here is a sixteen-measure progression. Use everything at your disposal to create a bass line. Even if you play things we haven't discussed, that's fine. There is much more to creating a walking line than we have learned. Learn what you can in advance, but when it's time to play, play!

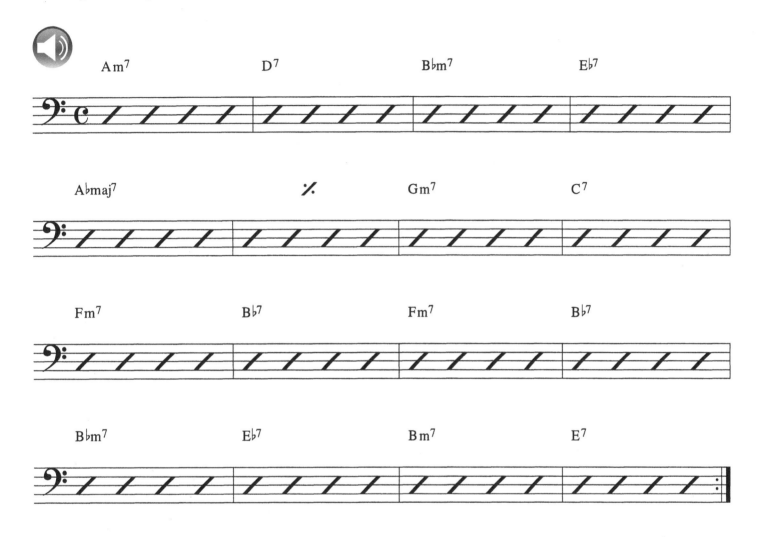

The Two Feel

Now that we have explored walking, let's take a step back. Walking is considered playing in "four" for obvious reasons. Playing in "two" is using half notes on beats one and three. This is an important approach to playing jazz, since many tunes start out in the "two" feel for the head, and go to "four" for the solos. Playing in two is also a common approach to playing "society" gigs. These are jobs that involve playing standard tunes, but with an emphasis on dancing. They are often considered "unhip" by many hard core jazz players, due to the lack of improvising, and medium tempos. Nevertheless, they can be a great way to learn the standard repertoire, and they generally pay much better than your average jazz gig. It is a fact that even Charlie Parker was known to play a wedding or two in his day! Still, for the bassist, these gigs will find you stuck in "two feel" most of the night, so let's take a look.

To successfully play in two is very simple. With one chord per measure, play the root on beat one, and the fifth on beat three. If there are two (or more) chords per measure, play the root on the downbeat of each new chord. Very simple. However, it takes a little discipline to stick with this. Avoid the temptation to "take it out," and you'll keep the gig. Here is an example of what I call the "straight two."

The straight two is the best thing to play when people are trying to dance "society style." Too much activity in the bass line makes it difficult for the dancers. Remember, this is not a funk gig! The straight two is also the basis of playing Latin styles, country & western, certain rock grooves, gospel, and many types of folk music from around the world. This is one reason that bass players can cross over the stylistic "barriers" of music so well. What we play is very much the same in many different idioms.

In a jazz context, we would want to be less restricted in our two feel. It is possible to expand on the two feel without becoming too overbearing. To do this, we use rhythmic embellishments, tastefully applied to give the line a more active role. Here is the same progression from before, but now with an expanded two feel.

As you can see from the previous example, it is important to strike a balance between activity and space. To avoid becoming an overbearing presence, play less!

Playing in 3/4 Time

Playing in 3/4 is another important skill for the jazz bassist. There is more to it than just walking and leaving out one beat per measure. With three beats per bar, your sense of phrasing changes. There are also alternatives to walking in "three." The first approach is playing in "one." Basically, we play only on the downbeat of each measure. This gives the tune an open "waltz-like" quality.

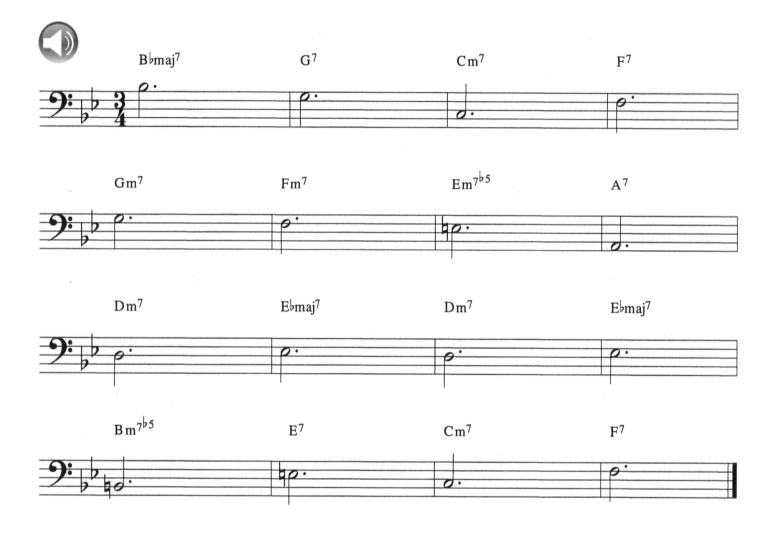

The next choice we have is the "two-over-three" feel. As the name suggests, we play in two, while the count is in three. If we divide a measure of 3/4 exactly in half, we have two dotted quarter notes. This will give us our two feel. This approach creates a unique polyrhythmic feel. This division of the time is useful when there are two chord changes in a measure of 3/4. It is also possible to play with the groove in this feel, and make the tune sound like it's in a slower 4/4. This concept was taken to great heights by Ron Carter and Tony Williams, with the Miles Davis Quintet. As long as you keep the form, you can really take this idea out! Another approach to this feel is to play a half note on beat one, and a quarter note on beat three.

This example takes the same progression from the previous example and uses the "two-over-three" feel.

The last approach for 3/4 is to simply walk in three. All the concepts of walking apply except that we need to phrase according to the number of beats in the measure. One melodic approach that works well in 3/4 is to use the triad of the chord as our walking line. There are three notes in the triad, and three notes in the measure. If you can smoothly lead into the next chord change this technique is very effective. Here is the same progression with a walking feel.

It is common to use all these ideas in the same tune when playing in 3/4. We may start the head out with a combination of "one" and "two-over-three" and then go to "three" for solos. Some tunes have sections that suggest a certain feel, and we may gravitate to it whenever that part of the song is reached. Here is the complete form of the tune used for the last three examples. Its form is AABA with the A sections being sixteen measures long. The bridge (B section) is eight measures long. The final A section ends with the second ending. This example will be one chorus (one time through the form) and will use all the different 3/4 approaches.

Latin

Latin music has always been a major ingredient in the jazz recipe. Dizzy Gillespie brought the Afro-Cuban influence into prominence with his collaborations with Machito back in the 1940's. Earlier, the Latin influence was present from the music's roots in New Orleans, a city where African, Caribbean, European, and South American cultures all blended with American styles to formulate what we now call jazz.

Just as there are many different types of jazz, there are many different styles of Latin music. "Latin" has become a very generic term in jazz circles. Almost anything that is even eighths instead of Swing eighth notes can be referred to as "Latin." Of course, this does injustice to the many unique forms of Latin music. Musical styles from Brazil and Puerto Rico, while sharing some similarities, are very different, particularly from the bass player's standpoint. Yet, they are both stuck under the heading of Latin. In a jazz context "Latin" usually means a derivative of bossa nova or samba, both styles from Brazil. This is due largely to the popularity brought to these styles by Stan Getz, exemplified by his recordings with famous Brazilian composer Antonio Carlos Jobim. Perhaps the most famous of all Jobim tunes, "The Girl from Ipanema" was a big hit for Getz, and ushered in a whole new desire to play jazz over this type of feel. Due to the universal appeal of jazz, there are many great artists from different Latin cultures playing jazz mixed with the rhythmic feel of their own country. To be realistic, it would take an entire book to explore all the various types of Latin jazz (there are several good ones available). So, instead we will look at what are the most common forms of "Latin" playing in jazz. The bossa and samba feels are very popular in the jazz repertoire. To be honest, what gets called a samba on a jazz gig is usually a far cry from what you would hear in Rio De Janeiro. The Brazilian musical tradition is very rich and time honored, but most jazz players learn samba from second and third-hand sources. What non-Brazilian jazz players call samba is not quite true to the roots of the music. In any case, we will learn to play what most American jazz players have come to call bossa, and samba.

Most Latin music is based on the two feel. The most common rhythmic approach is the dotted quarter note followed by an eighth note. This is used for both bossa and samba, the only difference being that samba is faster. Here is a short progression with the typical bossa feel.

Another approach to the bossa is to cut back even more and just play half notes. This may seem incredibly boring on the surface, but you may be surprised by how much this approach can groove with the right touch. Playing only half notes helps the music breathe. Latin music is very rhythmic, and cutting back on our own rhythmic input helps create space for the percussionist to really lay it down. In Brazilian music, there is a slight emphasis on the half-time back beat. This translates to beat three in a measure of 4/4. Play this example again, using only half notes with a subtle accent on beat three.

This next example is the American jazz version of the samba feel. It is essentially the bossa feel sped up, but the faster tempo does affect melodic and rhythmic choices. It is important that what you play lays well under the hands. If the line is awkward to play, it won't sound natural. If you get too active, it will not settle into the groove. Although you may have heard records with people such as Jaco Pastorious and Stanley Clarke playing this feel and throwing in lots of notes, bear in mind two things: 1. you are not either of them, and 2. you may lose your gig if you try to be like them. If it's your gig, I suppose you can play any way you want, but if you are hired by someone else, you're better off playing less notes. This is my opinion. Some people will undoubtedly disagree, but I know it works for me. Again, put a slight emphasis on beat three and it will feel more authentic.

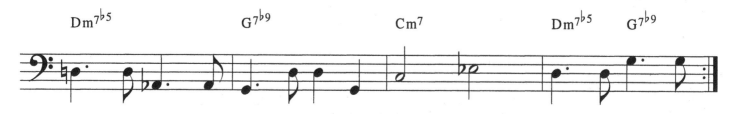

Now go back and play the previous example with only half notes. This is my preference; I think it lets the groove settle more. Of course, you can add some other things to the line, but use the half note as your starting point, and be economical.

Latin/Swing

No, this is not a new style played to accompany the merengue-lindy dance step, it is a common feel change used in some jazz tunes. Usually the A section will be played Latin style, and the bridge goes to a Swing feel. Many tunes have become known for being played this way, such as "Green Dolphin Street," or "Night and Day." Other tunes have been specifically written with feel changes in them, such as Cedar Walton's "Bolivia," which goes from swing to Latin and back again.

Executing these feel changes seamlessly requires a few things. First, we must know how each feel works, and, second, we must pay attention to the transition area. The transition area extends approximately two to three measures in front of the feel change, to one or two measures after the change. It is crucial to set up the feel change in your mind before you get there. This way you are prepared for it. You also need to play something that will set up the change as well. The drummer shares this responsibility. Depending on the tempo of the tune, you need to become aware of the shift approximately two or three measures ahead of it. This entails simply reminding yourself that it is coming. Next, in the one or two bars before the shift, you will react to it by playing something that reflects the change. Most often, it only takes one bar to set up the shift, but a drummer may want to use two bars. Going from Latin to swing, the most common thing to do is to start walking during the transition. Going back from swing to Latin, it is possible to continue walking through the transition and just switch back at the point of change. Alternatively, you can set it up by playing a Latin feel during the transition area. After the point of change, continue with the new feel focusing on smoothing out the flow, letting it settle in. The essential quality that changes at the shift point is the subdivision of the rhythmic flow. Latin style is based on a straight eighth-note feel, this is also known as duple meter (divisible by two). Swing is triple meter (divisible by three), using eighth-note triplets as its sub-pulse. This rhythmic change is at the core of the transition from Latin to swing.

Here is a short example of the Latin/swing transition. We are taking it from the last eight measures before the bridge. We will do the transition into the bridge and back out to the last eight measures of Latin. Pay attention to how the drums set up the rhythmic shift.

Remember, even though the subdivision changes, there is a consistent pulse that runs through both feels. Imagine a wire that is encased in a black coating. Then imagine the coating changing to orange, and then back to black. The wire that runs through the center is the inner core, the tempo that stays consistent even though the outer layers change.

37

Now you will have an opportunity to practice the Latin/Swing feel change over the complete tune. This song has an AABA form with the A sections being Latin, and the B section Swing. Pay attention to the transition areas, as each one will be a little different. Listen to how the drums set up the feel change, and how the bass reacts with it.

Latin

| Cmaj7 | Am7 | Dm7 | G7 | Cmaj7 | | Cm7 | F7 |

| B♭maj7 | | Em7♭5 | A7♭9 | Dmaj7 | | Dm7 | G7 |

| Cmaj7 | Am7 | Dm7 | G7 | Cmaj7 | | Cm7 | F7 |

| B♭maj7 | | Em7♭5 | A7♭9 | Dmaj7 | | Dm7 | G7 |

Swing

| Fmaj7 | | ⁒ | | Fm7 | | B♭7 | |

| E♭maj7 | | ⁒ | | Dm7 | | G7 | |

Latin

| Cmaj7 | Am7 | Dm7 | G7 | Cmaj7 | | Cm7 | F7 |

| B♭maj7 | | Em7♭5 | A7♭9 | Dmaj7 | | Dm7 | G7 |

| Cmaj7 | | B♭7 | A7 | Dm7 | G7 | Cmaj7 | |

Ballads

Playing a ballad is another important skill for the jazz bassist to learn. Ballads require a level of finesse and sensitivity that presents a real challenge for many bassists. The first goal of ballad playing is to support the tune without taking focus away from the melody. There is room for small statements here and there. (After all, we don't want to become totally invisible.) However, if people are listening to the bass player instead of the lead instrument, then the bassist is playing too much (or maybe the lead isn't very interesting, which is not your fault). When accompanying a ballad, every note is very exposed. There can be no questionable choices here. Play the roots, chord tones, and use approach types and passing tones to land on a strong choice in the right place. Play big, fat whole notes and half notes. Don't be afraid to hit the root on beat one and let it ring for the entire measure. Let the tone of the bass shine through. It's possible to say a lot with just one note. If you play upright or fretless bass, ballads are a great opportunity to "work" the note by adjusting your finger pressure. You can make a note "spread" by squeezing it with the left hand just after you attack the string. This takes some practice, but you can eventually learn to control the swelling. To a lesser extent, this technique can be achieved on fretted basses. On fretted instruments, the right-hand attack has a greater effect on the sound. Play ballads with the right hand close to the fingerboard, and point the plucking finger toward the bridge so you can use more of the flesh. The more meat you put on the string, the fatter your sound.

Vibrato is another technique that makes ballad playing more musical. Vibrato is achieved in two ways. The first is by shaking the left hand, letting it pivot off the finger that is holding the note down. The second is to slide the finger holding the note to subtly change the pitch back and forth. This technique works only on non-fretted instruments. Speed and width are very important aspects of vibrato. Practice getting a slow, controlled vibrato that is wide enough to hear, but not so wide that you can drive a truck through it! Fast vibrato has its uses, but not in ballad playing. As in our note choices, use the vibrato tastefully; we don't want to overdo it.

Here is an example of ballad playing. Notice how the line is balanced with whole, half, quarter and, occasionally eighth notes. Pay attention to how the tone of the bass says more than the actual notes.

Soloing

Taking a solo is another skill the jazz bassist must have. After backing up everyone else's solo, it comes time for your statement. The bass presents certain inherent challenges for the budding soloist, but these challenges have been met, and mastered, since the early 1930s when Jimmy Blanton played with Duke Ellington. Modern masters like Paul Chambers, Scot LaFaro, Jaco Pastorious, and many others have pushed the art of the bass solo to amazingly high standards.

Taking a solo can be an intimidating prospect for the bassist for several reasons. First, the bassist's primary role is that of an accompanist. We spend the bulk of our time learning how to be a rhythm section player. The challenge of that task alone is sufficient to keep a new bassist busy for years. Bassists have enough work to do to become a functional member of the musical community that learning to solo tends to take a back seat. Second, how we initially learn to approach harmony is by connecting the root motion. This is very practical for us as accompanist, but as soloists, it leaves us "root bound." It takes some re-orientation for the bassist to look at chord changes in ways that will help create a melodic solo. Third, low frequencies are naturally harder to hear, so projecting your solo to the forefront is a sonic challenge. Fourth, soloing demands an even greater degree of technical mastery. While we spend the majority of our jazz time playing quarter notes, the solo generally involves playing eighth notes, eighth-note triplets, sixteenth-notes, maybe even sixteenth-note triplets. Fifth, because we stop walking to solo, the entire feel of the rhythm section changes. This helps us by creating the sonic space needed for a bass solo to exist, but it also can be unsettling at first. Sometimes, the other rhythm section players rely so heavily on the bassist to keep things together, when you stop walking to take your solo, they may get lost, skip a beat, or even stop playing completely (in my opinion, this is preferable to the first two situations.) To be fair, these things can happen to the bassist attempting a solo as well. With all of these challenges set before you, it is possible to become discouraged. Instead, listen to some Eddie Gomez and get inspired!

Soloing is a *big* topic, and due to the introductory nature of this book, it can not be dealt with in a comprehensive manner. However, what I will do is give an overview of the skills needed to take a solo, discuss some basic strategies for creating a melodic statement, play some examples of a bass soloing and give you space to practice taking a solo yourself. This will give you a basic idea of what must be done. Learning to take a good bass solo requires a lot of preparation, so be patient, and give yourself permission to make mistakes.

Preparing to Solo

Taking a solo is like telling a story. The events you are describing are the chord changes, the melody, the rhythm, and how you feel about them. If you want to tell a good story, then you have to know what you are talking about. First, you must know the chord structures. Earlier in this book you were presented with a list of commonly used chord structures. If you are not completely familiar with them, go back and study them. Play each chord type up and down, and in as many places on the fingerboard as you can find. Pay attention to the unique sound that each chord type has.

Each chord structure also has a corresponding scale. Often you have more than one possible scale for each chord. Here is a list of the chord types we have discussed with their corresponding scale structures. The minor seventh chord has three different scales listed. Which scale you choose is based on whether the chord is a IIm7, IIIm7, or VIm7 in the key.

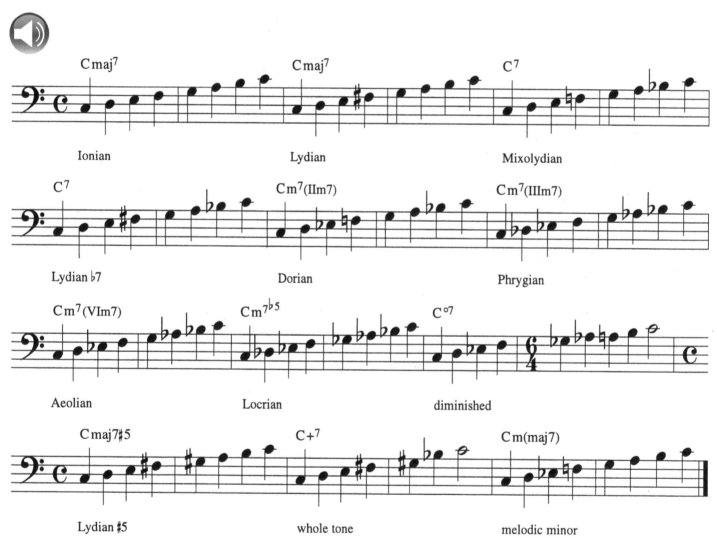

Now that you have familiarized yourself with the chord and scale structures, we will look at a simple but effective way to get to melodic material for soloing. A common challenge bassists face when taking a solo is getting away from the root motion. When we accompany other musicians, it serves us well to outline the root motion. However when we solo, this can be uninteresting. If we learn to look at the chord progression from the third of each chord, we are instantly thrust into a new layer of the harmony. The lines we create off the third are more melodic because they relate to a more colorful place in the chord structure.

Here is a standard chord progression in B♭ with its corresponding scales and arpeggios built off the root. The scale for the G7 is an Aeolian scale with a natural third to match the chord structure. This chord contains a B natural which does not belong to the key of B♭.

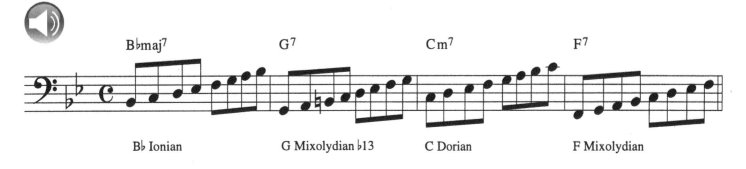

Next, determine the third of each chord: for B♭maj7, it's D; for G7, it's B; for Cm7, it's E♭; and for F7, it's A. This will become our new root motion. By building up in thirds from these notes we will get a new chord progression. This progression works with the original one because we still have three quarters of the structures in use. The old chord structure was root, third, fifth, seventh. Our new chord will be third, fifth, seventh, ninth. Here is the new progression, built from the thirds of the original progression.

These are the scales that correspond to the new progression. The B altered scale in the second measure is a result of a B natural being transplanted into the key of B♭. You will play the new material, while the pianist plays the original changes. Listen to how melodic these new scales sound.

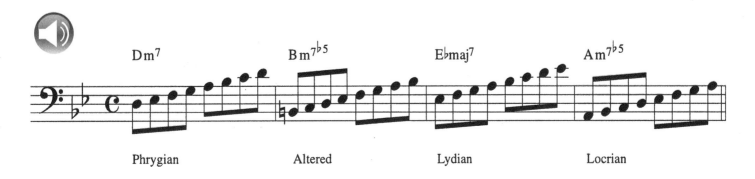

43

In addition to the scale material, also learn the new arpeggios built from the thirds of our original progression. Playing the new arpeggio up from the third lands you on the ninth of the original chord. The ninth is actually the second scale degree from the root, only up an octave. This is a very interesting note to emphasize. Again, the pianist will play the original progression.

Now that you have some melodic material to work with, we have to put it into action musically. Learning how to phrase your ideas so they make musical sense is a long-term process. We can start by working with small groups of notes. Short motifs can be very effective and musical if developed. We can take a short phrase and use the basic shape through the progression, switching to the corresponding scale or arpeggio for each chord change. Here are some motifs we can play with.

Obviously there is quite a bit more we can do, but, for now, we will have to move on to other things. In the near future I will be writing an in-depth book about soloing. Until then, there are many other texts available to give you more information. Remember, when it's time to take your solo, concentrate on hearing your ideas before you play them. Use space; it's not necessary to fill up every beat. Pay attention to how you finish your solo; at the end, you will have to go back to a walking bass line. Planning ahead will make for a smooth transition.

Here is an opportunity to solo over a blues in B♭. On a separate sheet of paper, write out the chord changes built from the thirds. The B♭7 chord becomes a Dm7♭5, the E♭7 becomes Gm7♭5, Dm7 becomes Fmaj7, G7 becomes Bm7♭5, Cm7 becomes E♭maj7, and F7 becomes Am7♭5. Writing out the new changes is a good way to learn to see them on your own. Eventually you will look at a set of changes and be able to see the many layers that exist. This example will give you two choruses to solo, then return to walk for one chorus. This is to give you practice ending your solo and getting back to walking.

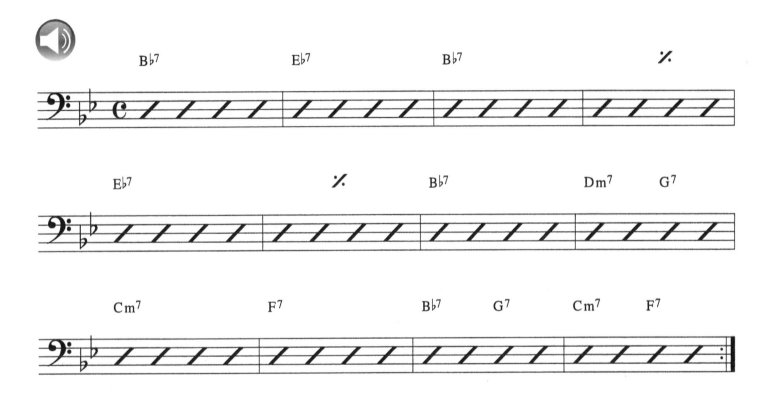

Part Two

In this section we will learn about performance format. When a group gets together to play jazz, there is protocol that exists to ensure that things run smoothly. Each player is responsible for understanding the role of his instrument within the group, and how the group will function. Throughout the history of jazz, there have been many groups that carved out new rules for themselves, looking to go beyond the standard format and create something unique. Much can be learned by studying the music of these ground breakers, for they are directly responsible for the evolution of the music. Among the most influential musicians are Charlie Parker, Dizzy Gillespie, Thelonius Monk (especially their early bop configurations), Miles Davis, John Coltrane, and Ornette Coleman. Along with countless others, they reworked the standard performance format to create new ways of approaching jazz.

It is a very common occurrence in jazz to have a group of total strangers get together to play, totally unrehearsed, on a gig in front of a live audience. While this may sound extremely risky, if the players are experienced they will all know standard performance protocol. This enables players that have never met, from all corners of the world, to get together and make music.

Performance Protocol

The most basic format used to perform a jazz tune is: head, solos, head again, and out (end the tune). There are variations on this theme, but, essentially, that is the basis of all standard jazz performances. A common variation is to add an intro (introduction) to the head. The intro may be comprised of material from the tune about to be played, or perhaps a simple pedal point on the dominant (fifth) of the key, or, in some cases, may be a miniature composition in its own right. Here are a few of the most common intros.

Intros

The first intro we will look at is the vamp. This is used quite often, particularly if you are making a segue from another tune, a common practice on "society" gigs. A vamp is a short progression that is repeated until a cue is given to move on to the next section, in this case, the head. The most common vamp is the I-VI-II-V progression, usually in the same key as the tune about to be played. A variant of that would be III-VI-II-V. intros are usually four or eight measures, depending sometimes on the tempo of the tune. If the tune is slow, eight measures will feel too long; for a ballad, two measures may be sufficient. Here is an eight-measure vamp intro that incorporates the I-VI-II-V and the III-VI-II-V progressions. Notice how the band sets up the top of the form in the last measure. There will be four measures of the head played before the fade out.

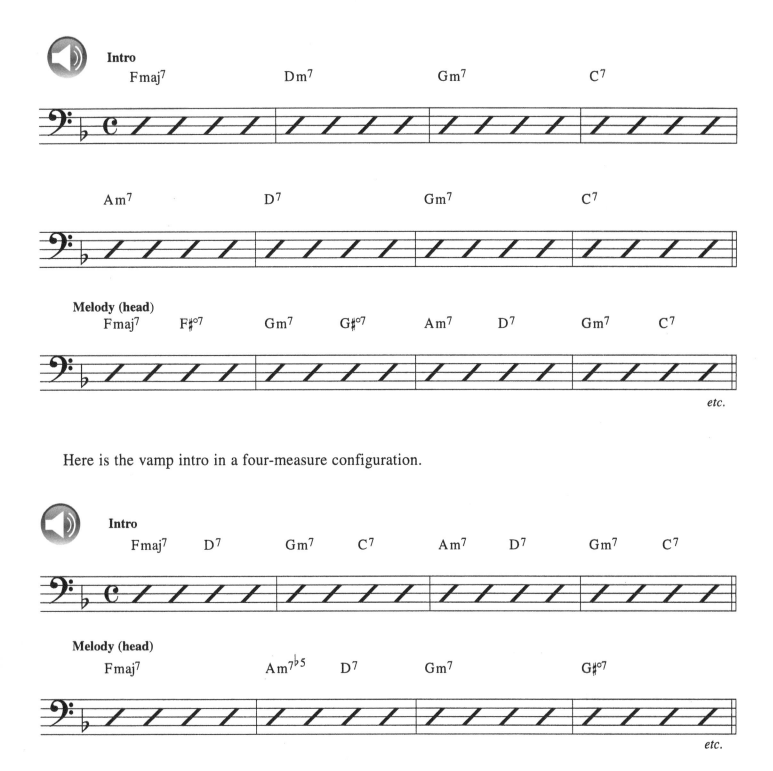

Here is the vamp intro in a four-measure configuration.

Another common intro is the dominant pedal. The dominant is the fifth of the key, so if the tune is in B♭, the dominant pedal would be F. The pedal can be a rhythmic figure, or a sustained note, most often, played on beats two and four. The latter is often referred to as "pedal on the five, two and four." Here it is.

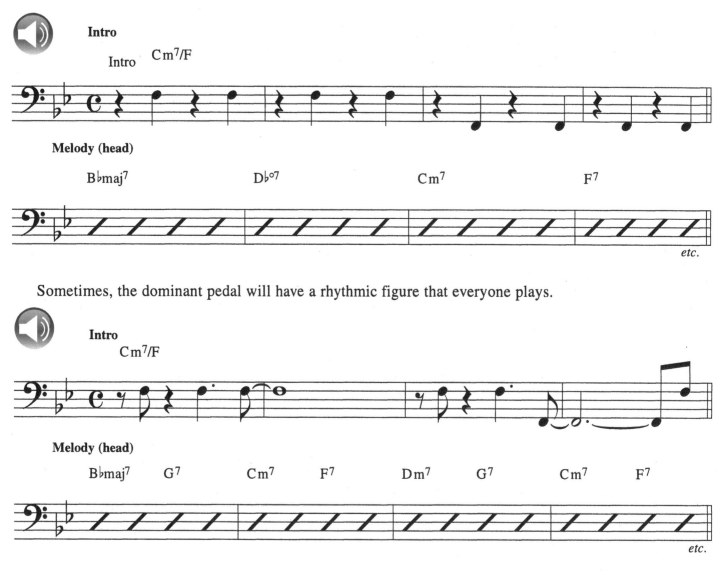

Sometimes, the dominant pedal will have a rhythmic figure that everyone plays.

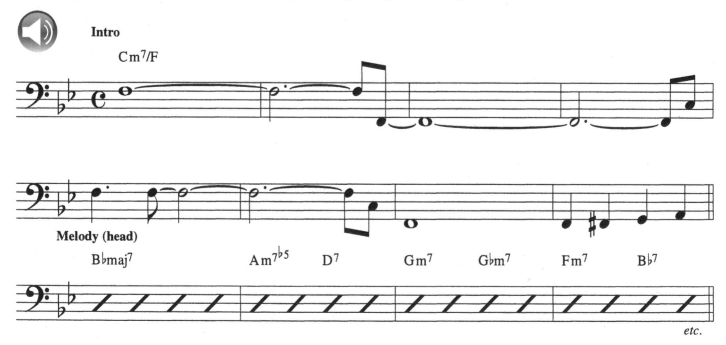

Here is a sustained dominant pedal. Notice how, in the last measure of the intro, the bass starts walking. This helps get the tune moving after sitting on the pedal point for eight measures.

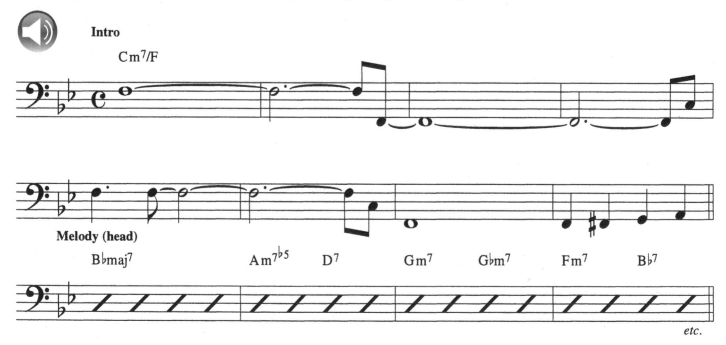

Another common intro is the last four or eight measures of the tune. This works well because most tunes are composed in such a way that the end of the form sets up the top. These intros are commonly referred to as "last four" or "last eight." Here is an example of "last eight." The last measure of the intro is the turn around that sets up the top.

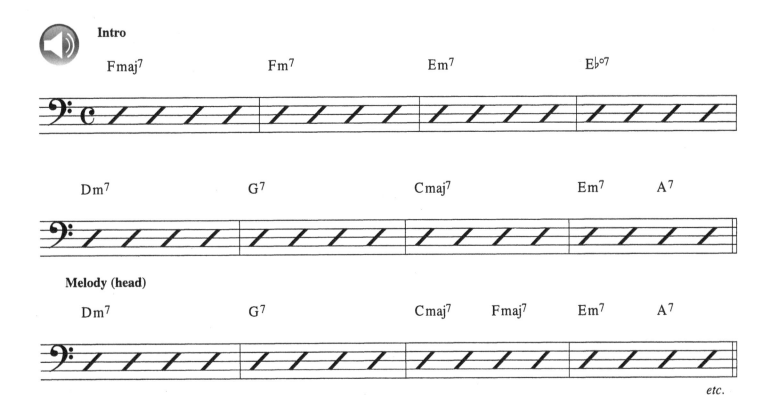

Aside from the previous examples, there are intros comprised of material distinct from the actual tune. These intros generally belong to a specific tune. A well-known example is the classic Charlie Parker intro to "All the Things You Are." There are too many other examples to list; the only way you'll learn them is by listening and playing.

Endings

Now that we've discussed intros, the next thing to learn is how to end a tune. If you have a good intro and a solid ending, the band sounds great to most people regardless of what happens in the middle. This is not to suggest that the middle of a tune is unimportant, quite the opposite. What I mean is that the intro and ending are the parts of a performance most listeners can recall. This is based in the mechanics of how memory works. So, if the band sounds great, but the ending gets messed up, you have left the audience with that messed-up ending as a lasting impression. Most educated jazz audiences will forgive a less-than-tidy ending if the playing that preceded it was brilliant. Hopefully, you will be lucky enough to play brilliantly in front of an educated jazz audience. Either way, it's a good idea to learn the ending.

There are a number of ways to end a tune. Some tunes have specific endings built into the composition. These will take the form of a coda, which is an extra section of music added on to the end of a piece that brings the music to a final cadence. These must be learned tune by tune, for they are specific to the composition. There are a great many "stock" endings that exist, as well as strategies for putting them into action.

This next example is the all-time classic stock ending. It is generally used in place of the last two measures of the form.

This ending is the basis of countless variations. The common factor in all of them is a rhythmic emphasis on the following beats.

Sometimes this ending gets a stinger on the end.

50

Sometimes the stinger is held long. During the hold, the drummer will usually play a fill, and make it obvious when everyone should catch a "bump" on the end to "seal off" the tune. The best approach for this situation is to let your note ring while everyone else is going crazy, and stop it on the "bump."

Sometimes these additional kicks show up after the hold.

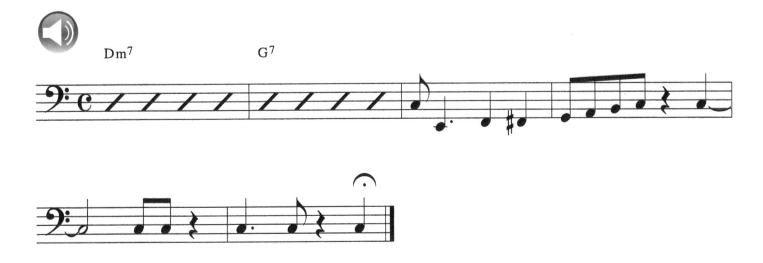

Sometimes, the kicks are extended even farther!

This variation uses the rhythmic idea, but avoids the actual line cliché. This works well as a generic ending because everyone knows where the rhythmic kicks are, yet the pianist or horn players can still improvise something to end the tune.

This next one is referred to as the "Basie" ending (as in Count Basie).

This ending is slightly extended, and uses a descending chromatic progression from the ♯IVm7♭5 chord. This is sometimes called the "#4" ending.

This is an extended "#4" ending.

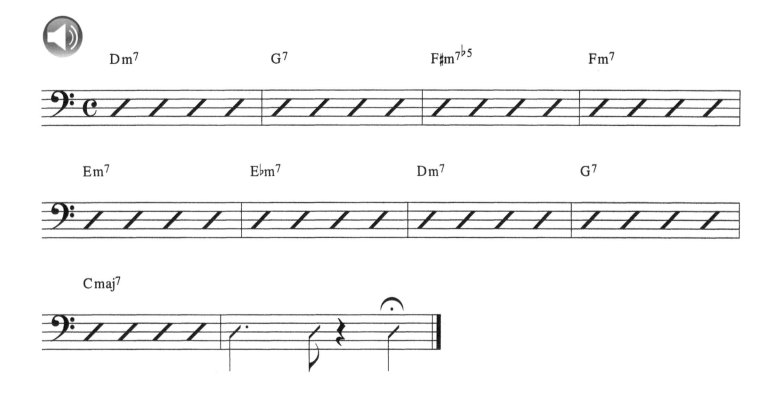

There are times where the ending of a tune may be built into the melody. If there is a melodic figure at the end of a tune, it often gets used as the ending, particularly if it is rhythmic. This example is the last eight bars of a tune. The written music is the melody, in treble clef. Walk through the changes, and catch the kick with the last melody note. Be sure to play the root of the Cmaj7 chord on the "and" of beat four. This is known as "anticipating the downbeat."

Another common practice for ending a tune is to extend the form. Some of the previous examples used extensions of the form, but the common "triple-tag" ending uses the last four measures as its extension. This example will show you the triple tag written out. Bear in mind that this ending is not usually written. It is most often executed by an unspoken agreement. The cue for this ending is the IIIm7-VI7 turnaround or just the VI7 chord thrown in the last measure. Again, the written music is the melody. Keep walking through the measures that have whole rests in them. Catch the last kick with the melody.

Sometimes, the tag ending will extend for quite a while. At the end of the tune, someone will start improvising over the tag, and keep it going until they cue the real ending. The tag has been known to go on for as long as an entire tune! If someone starts to "blow" (improvise) when you get to the tag, be prepared to hang with it for a while. It should be made obvious through a musical or visual cue when to go to the ending.

Standard Performance Format

There are many possibilities for a jazz performance. The essence of the music lends itself to experimentation. Yet, due to the somewhat transient nature of the jazz life, it is common for a group of strangers to show up at a club, and have to play like a band without the benefit of rehearsal. In fact, many musicians prefer not to rehearse for jazz gigs because they feel it takes away from the freshness of the music. There are arguments that support this theory and others that refute it. However, if musicians are going to just show up and play somewhere, they must have a set of standard procedures to keep things somewhat organized.

The standard performance format runs down like this: 1. a tune is called, 2. the tune is counted off, 3. there will most likely be an intro of some sort, 4. the head is played. (If the tune is a blues, or a relatively short form, the head is played twice. Thirty-two measure forms, like AABA, are played only once), 5. Solos over the form begin (the typical hierarchy in jazz is horn players—or any lead instrument—solo first, then the rhythm section which would be piano and/or guitar, bass, and finally drums [generally, drummers and often bass players will not solo on every tune]), 6. if the drums do solo, the head will follow (played once or twice depending on how many times it was played at the top), 7. after the head, some sort of ending will occur, either by prior agreement, or by someone taking charge and making it happen.

Each of these events requires some attention on your part. For things to run smoothly, it is very important that the rhythm-section players pay attention to the format. After a while, you will be so experienced, you will not have to think about it too much. It becomes an instinctual process. Until then, know what is coming up so you are prepared to make a smooth transition.

Playing behind the different soloists requires subtle shifts in the energy. Backing up a trumpet solo feels different than playing behind a tenor sax solo. A piano solo has a different feel than a guitar solo. Of course, the individual doing the playing has the most to do with how we accompany them. If someone is starting out mellow, building up to something big, we want to work with that idea. It's not a good idea to bulldoze your way through someone's rose garden. Listen to the soloist and go with them. There is an essential give and take that needs to occur. If the soloist isn't listening to the rhythm section, then the band starts to feel like they are just being used as a glorified play-along record.

Give the Drummer Some

After you've taken your brilliant bass solo, it's time for the drummer. There are a few ways to deal with this. One way is to simply stop at the end of your solo and give the drummer an "open" solo. This means the drummer plays unaccompanied over the same form everyone else did. Naturally, the drummer is not playing chords or melody, so it is important to keep the sound of the tune in your head during the drum solo; sing the melody to yourself. This is the best way to make sure there is no doubt about where the band comes in after the drum solo. Sometimes, the drum solo becomes really "open," and the drummer plays without keeping the form. In such instances it is up to the drummer to wind down the solo and then give some type of well-placed cue to get everyone back to the top of the form.

Another common approach for the drum solo is called "trading fours." After the last solo (often the bass), someone will start to improvise. They play for four measures and stop, giving the next four to the drums. Everyone takes a turn trading four-measure phrases with the drummer. However, the bass player usually does not get into the trading. If you get "the look" from someone, that will signal you to trade as well. Trading fours can be very exciting, each soloist gets to interact with the drummer, playing off each other's ideas. It is good to pay careful attention to the drums during fours. Even some of the best drummers in the world have been known to "stretch" their four measures a little. Sometimes their rhythmic phrasing doesn't end up exactly where you would expect. So listen and watch; it's important to hit on the downbeat together. Generally, drummers keep the hi-hat "chicking" on beats two and four during their solos. Lock in with this and you will have no problems determining where the downbeat is.

Here is an example of trading fours over a blues progression. The fours will last for two choruses, the end will be the downbeat of the third chorus.

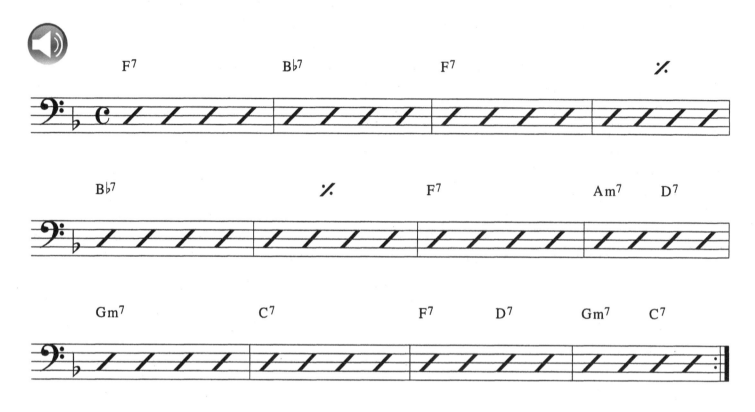

A variation on this theme is trading "eights." As you would expect, it works the same as "fours" except this time we trade eight-measure phrases. This requires a little more of your attention since you have to stay with the drummer twice as long. If the drummer has a tendency to obscure the downbeat, then trading eights can be quite risky. Besides locking in with the hi-hat, mentally mark the downbeats of each measure as it passes by counting up to eight. This is a good idea even if the drummer is very clear with the time because it will help you develop a strong instinct for eight-measure-phrase lengths.

Here is an example of trading eights. The thirty-two-measure progression will run only once through the form; the end will be the top of the second chorus.

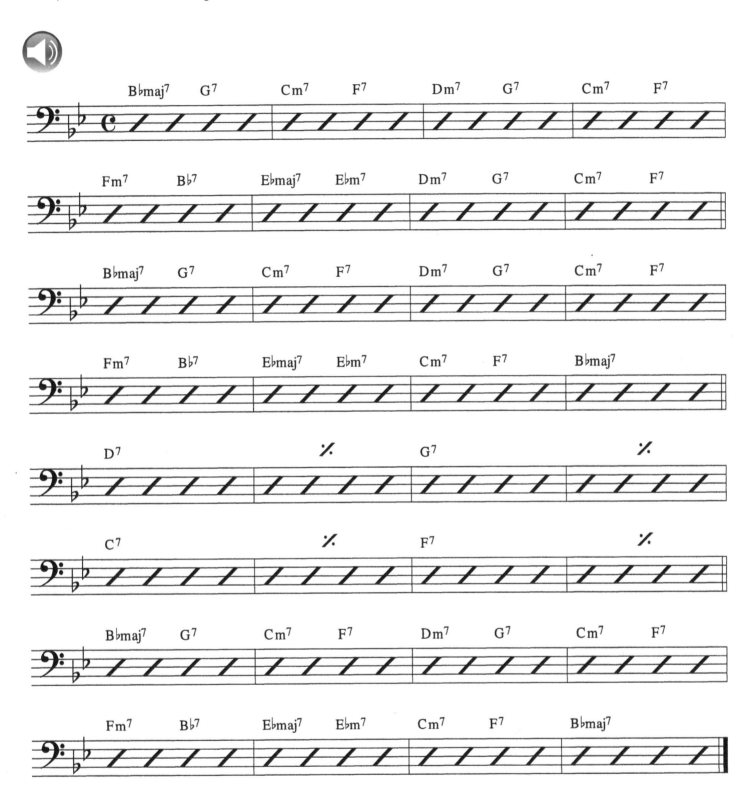

Occasionally, trading with the drums can lead to some exciting variations. Sometimes, the first chorus of trading will be eights, then the next chorus will be fours, then the next chorus will be twos! Trading ones can even be done, but it takes quite a bit of experience to make it sound good. Another fun variation on a twelve-measure blues is to split the chorus down the middle and trade sixes!

As you can see, trading with the drums can be quite interesting, particularly if you don't know in advance what will happen. These decisions are often made on the spot. If someone holds up four fingers at the end of the bass solo, that will be the cue to trade fours. Someone may just call out "eights," and off you go.

Putting It into Action

Now that we have dealt with most of what you need to be a functional bassist in a jazz context, it's time to use it. The following examples are intended to give you some experience dealing with a variety of situations. Mostly you will be looking at "lead sheets" which contain the chord changes and the melody. Although you are not playing the melody, it's good to have it in front of you to help keep your place in the form, give you ideas about how to approach the tune rhythmically and melodically, and, yes, it is not unheard of for the bass player to play the melody too. Of course, this means you'll have to learn how to read treble clef since most melody instruments are written in it. (For now, you may have your hands full doing everything you've just learned. If so, make reading treble clef a goal for the future; it can come in very handy.) Some of the lead sheets will have chord changes but no melody. This happens very often. Someone will scratch out the chords to a tune on a piece of paper (or a cocktail napkin) and give it to you to play. Not having the melody to look at forces you to listen even more closely in order to pick up on the form and kicks that may occur in the head. These lead sheets will contain only the form of the tune. Intros and endings will not be written out. If there is any specific information about the tune you must know, it will be told to you much in the way a band leader will tell you: short and sweet. The instructions will all be conveyed using "real jazz lingo." So, if you ain't hip, you just won't get it, dig? One important difference to make note of is the exchange of the term "bars" for "measures." While "measure" is the technically correct term, most musicians refer to them as "bars." Have fun with these, and good luck!

This first tune is a twelve bar blues in G, with an eight-bar piano intro on the five, head twice, two choruses apiece, trade fours after the bass solo, head out, with a short ending.

"Bad Shoes Blues"

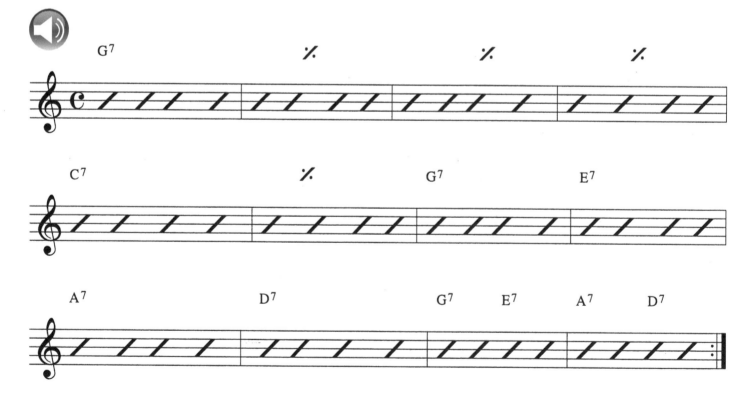

Time for a trio tune. This one is a thirty-two-bar ABCD form in the key of C. Play the head once through in two, walk for the solos (one chorus each), trade eight's with the drums one chorus, bass trades too. For the head out, the first half is in two, then go to four for the last half. Do a triple tag with a Basie ending.

"I Don't Care"

This one is Latin, in C minor. Head twice, two choruses for each solo. Triple tag with a ritard ending.

"Primary Color Bossa"

This tune is Latin/swing for the head, solos go to swing. One chorus apiece (trombone, sax, piano, and bass). After the bass solo, play the head out, then triple tag to a Latin vamp for the ending.

"Purple Porpoise Road"

It's 3/4 time. This trio tune has a dominant pedal intro for eight bars. The head is played once through in a "one" feel. The piano takes two choruses, bass one chorus, then bass and drums trade fours. The last four bars of the head start the intro vamp again. On cue, play flat two major seventh (Bmaj7) and resolve it to the one.

"Waiting for Kodak"

Now let's play a ballad. This is a short form, only ten bars long. The head is played once. Sax takes one chorus, piano takes one. One chorus of the head out, repeat the first three bars for the ending.

"Red and Yellow"

This last tune is a straight ahead bopper. AABA form, play the last four for the intro, head once through in and out. One chorus for horns and piano, (no bass solo), one chorus trading fours, catch the hit in bar thirty two for the ending.

"Cancellation"

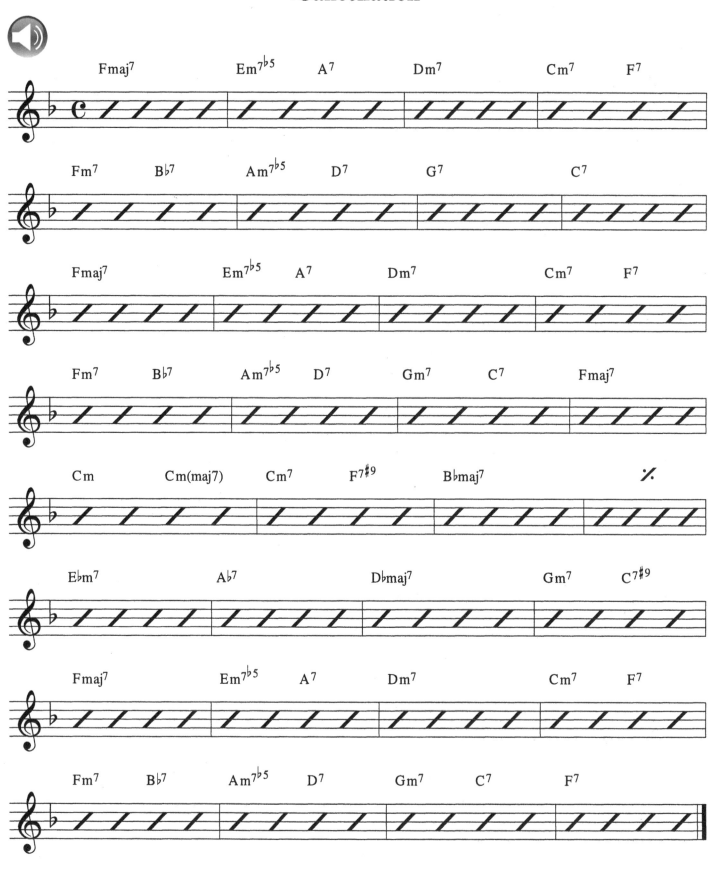

A Final Word

You have now covered most of what you need to know in order to go out into the jazz scene and function. I say "most of what you need" because the missing piece is the experience you'll get on the gig. Jazz started as a folkloric tradition. It was handed down through the generations by listening, watching, hanging out, maybe picking up a few pointers from an experienced pro in a good mood, and a lot of learning by trial and error on the gig. If you weren't making it, you'd be told pretty quickly. That essential "egg-on-your-face" experience has provided the necessary motivation for most of our great jazz artists, and you will be no different. Because you have worked through this book (and perhaps other books as well) doesn't mean you know everything you need to know. It is wise to approach the art of playing jazz with respect and humility; we all have a lot to learn. The great jazz artists in the world already know this, and that knowledge is what keeps them growing and searching. The day you think you've got it all together, is the day you stop learning. When that day comes, maybe you'll find your music being played on one of the many "smooth jazz" radio stations that pollute the airwaves, creating an unrealistic impression of what "jazz" is. Laying down a funky, good time, two chord groove to a computerized rhythm track while some whining anonymous sounding sax player bleats out insipid melodic fragments may be fun, and profitable, but it ain't jazz! But, you already knew that. From the lessons learned in this book you will have a good head start, so start swingin'!

Glossary of Terms

Through out this book I will use much of the common terminology of jazz. Some of these terms have made their way into the mainstream, however many of them may be new to you, or have different meanings than you are accustomed to. This glossary will clarify any terms you may not be familiar with.

A — short for "A section," the first part of the form of a tune.

B — short for "B section," the second part of the form of a tune, also called "the bridge."

Bar — measure

Bird — Charlie Parker

Bridge — the B section of the form, or the second part of the melody of a tune.

C — short for "C section," the third part of the form of a tune, not always present.

Chart — a lead sheet of a song containing the melody and chord changes. Sometimes only chord changes are written. Can be used to describe any piece of written music to be played. Also used to describe an arrangement for a tune. Ex. "I wrote a chart of 'Donna Lee' for the big band."

Chord Chart — see "Chart"

Chorus — another term for once through the form of a song

Eights — also "trading eights." Alternating eight bar phrases, usually with the drummer, "fours" and "twos" can also be traded.

Fours — also "trading fours," alternating four bar phrases, usually with the drummer.

Four — playing in 4/4 time, walking quarter notes on the bass.

Gig — a musical engagement, usually paid, though in jazz, money is not always involved. Also used to describe jam sessions or rehearsals if you're not doing anything else.

Head — the melody of a tune.

Kicks — rhythmic figures

Lead Sheet — a written chart of a song containing the melody and chord changes.

Ritard — slow down

Tonic — the key center of a piece. Ex. If a song is in the key of G major, then a Gmaj7 chord would be the tonic chord. Also referred to as the I (one) chord.

Top — the beginning of an arrangement, or the beginning of a song form as in "top of the form."

Trane — John Coltrane

Twelve bar — a twelve-bar blues progression

Two — playing in 2/2 time, playing half notes on the bass.

BASS BUILDERS

A series of technique book/audio packages created for the purposeful building and development of your chops. Each volume is written by an expert in that particular technique. And with the inclusion of audio, the added dimension of hearing exactly how to play particular grooves and techniques make these truly like private lessons.

BASS AEROBICS
by Jon Liebman
00696437 Book/Online Audio $19.99

**BASS FITNESS –
AN EXERCISING HANDBOOK**
by Josquin des Prés
00660177 .... $12.99

BASS FOR BEGINNERS
by Glenn Letsch
00695099 Book/CD Pack $19.95

BASS GROOVES
by Jon Liebman
00696028 Book/Online Audio $19.99

BASS IMPROVISATION
by Ed Friedland
00695164 Book/Online Audio $19.99

BLUES BASS
by Jon Liebman
00695235 Book/Online Audio $19.99

BUILDING WALKING BASS LINES
by Ed Friedland
00695008 Book/Online Audio $19.99

**RON CARTER –
BUILDING JAZZ BASS LINES**
00841240 Book/Online Audio $19.99

DICTIONARY OF BASS GROOVES
by Sean Malone
00695266 Book/Online Audio $14.95

EXPANDING WALKING BASS LINES
by Ed Friedland
00695026 Book/CD Pack $19.95

**FINGERBOARD HARMONY
FOR BASS**
by Gary Willis
00695043 Book/Online Audio $17.99

FUNK BASS
by Jon Liebman
00699348 Book/Online Audio $19.99

FUNK/FUSION BASS
by Jon Liebman
00696553 Book/CD Pack $19.95

HIP-HOP BASS
by Josquin des Prés
00695589 Book/CD Pack $15.99

JAZZ BASS
by Ed Friedland
00695084 Book/Online Audio $17.99

**JERRY JEMMOTT –
BLUES AND RHYTHM &
BLUES BASS TECHNIQUE**
00695176 Book/CD Pack $17.95

JUMP 'N' BLUES BASS
by Keith Rosier
00695292 Book/CD Pack $17.99

**THE LOST ART OF
COUNTRY BASS**
by Keith Rosier
00695107 Book/CD Pack $19.95

**PENTATONIC SCALES
FOR BASS**
by Ed Friedland
00696224 Book/Online Audio $19.99

REGGAE BASS
by Ed Friedland
00695163 Book/Online Audio $16.95

'70S FUNK & DISCO BASS
by Josquin des Prés
00695614 Book/Online Audio $16.99

**SIMPLIFIED SIGHT-READING
FOR BASS**
by Josquin des Prés
00695085 Book/Online Audio $17.99

6-STRING BASSICS
by David Gross
00695221 Book/Online Audio $14.99

HAL•LEONARD®
www.halleonard.com

Prices, contents and availability subject to change without notice; All prices are listed in U.S. funds

0518

Jazz Instruction & Improvisation

BOOKS FOR ALL INSTRUMENTS FROM HAL LEONARD

AN APPROACH TO JAZZ IMPROVISATION
by Dave Pozzi
Musicians Institute Press
Explore the styles of Charlie Parker, Sonny Rollins, Bud Powell and others with this comprehensive guide to jazz improvisation. Covers: scale choices • chord analysis • phrasing • melodies • harmonic progressions • more.
00695135 Book/CD Pack..$17.95

THE ART OF MODULATING
FOR PIANISTS AND JAZZ MUSICIANS
by Carlos Salzedo &
Lucile Lawrence
Schirmer
The Art of Modulating is a treatise originally intended for the harp, but this edition has been edited for use by intermediate keyboardists and other musicians who have an understanding of basic music theory. In its pages you will find: table of intervals; modulation rules; modulation formulas; examples of modulation; extensions and cadences; ten fragments of dances; five characteristic pieces; and more.
50490581 ....$19.99

BUILDING A JAZZ VOCABULARY
By Mike Steinel
A valuable resource for learning the basics of jazz from Mike Steinel of the University of North Texas. It covers: the basics of jazz • how to build effective solos • a comprehensive practice routine • and a jazz vocabulary of the masters.
00849911 ....$19.99

THE CYCLE OF FIFTHS
by Emile and Laura De Cosmo
This essential instruction book provides more than 450 exercises, including hundreds of melodic and rhythmic ideas. The book is designed to help improvisors master the cycle of fifths, one of the primary progressions in music. Guaranteed to refine technique, enhance improvisational fluency, and improve sight-reading!
00311114 ....$16.99

THE DIATONIC CYCLE
by Emile and Laura De Cosmo
Renowned jazz educators Emile and Laura De Cosmo provide more than 300 exercises to help improvisors tackle one of music's most common progressions: the diatonic cycle. This book is guaranteed to refine technique, enhance improvisational fluency, and improve sight-reading!
00311115 ....$16.95

EAR TRAINING
by Keith Wyatt,
Carl Schroeder and Joe Elliott
Musicians Institute Press
Covers: basic pitch matching • singing major and minor scales • identifying intervals • transcribing melodies and rhythm • identifying chords and progressions • seventh chords and the blues • modal interchange, chromaticism, modulation • and more.
00695198 Book/Online Audio $24.99

EXERCISES AND ETUDES FOR THE JAZZ INSTRUMENTALIST
by J.J. Johnson
Designed as study material and playable by any instrument, these pieces run the gamut of the jazz experience, featuring common and uncommon time signatures and keys, and styles from ballads to funk. They are progressively graded so that both beginners and professionals will be challenged by the demands of this wonderful music.
00842018 Bass Clef Edition $19.99
00842042 Treble Clef Edition $16.95

JAZZOLOGY
THE ENCYCLOPEDIA OF JAZZ THEORY FOR ALL MUSICIANS
by Robert Rawlins and
Nor Eddine Bahha
This comprehensive resource covers a variety of jazz topics, for beginners and pros of any instrument. The book serves as an encyclopedia for reference, a thorough methodology for the student, and a workbook for the classroom.
00311167 ....$19.99

JAZZ THEORY RESOURCES
by Bert Ligon
Houston Publishing, Inc.
This is a jazz theory text in two volumes. **Volume 1 includes**: review of basic theory • rhythm in jazz performance • triadic generalization • diatonic harmonic progressions and analysis • substitutions and turnarounds • and more. **Volume 2 includes**: modes and modal frameworks • quartal harmony • extended tertian structures and triadic superimposition • pentatonic applications • coloring "outside" the lines and beyond • and more.
00030458 Volume 1 ....$39.99
00030459 Volume 2 ....$32.99

HAL•LEONARD®
7777 W. BLUEMOUND RD. P.O. BOX 13819 MILWAUKEE, WI 53213

Visit Hal Leonard online at
www.halleonard.com

JOY OF IMPROV
by Dave Frank
and John Amaral
This book/audio course on improvisation for all instruments and all styles will help players develop monster musical skills! Book One imparts a solid basis in technique, rhythm, chord theory, ear training and improv concepts. **Book Two** explores more advanced chord voicings, chord arranging techniques and more challenging blues and melodic lines. The audio can be used as a listening and play-along tool.
00220005 Book 1 – Book/Online Audio...............$27.99
00220006 Book 2 – Book/Online Audio...............$26.99

THE PATH TO JAZZ IMPROVISATION
by Emile and Laura De Cosmo
This fascinating jazz instruction book offers an innovative, scholarly approach to the art of improvisation. It includes in-depth analysis and lessons about: cycle of fifths • diatonic cycle • overtone series • pentatonic scale • harmonic and melodic minor scale • polytonal order of keys • blues and bebop scales • modes • and more.
00310904 ....$19.99

THE SOURCE
THE DICTIONARY OF CONTEMPORARY AND TRADITIONAL SCALES
by Steve Barta
This book serves as an informative guide for people who are looking for good, solid information regarding scales, chords, and how they work together. It provides right and left hand fingerings for scales, chords, and complete inversions. Includes over 20 different scales, each written in all 12 keys.
00240885 ....$19.99

21 BEBOP EXERCISES
by Steve Rawlins
This book/CD pack is both a warm-up collection and a manual for bebop phrasing. Its tasty and sophisticated exercises will help you develop your proficiency with jazz interpretation. It concentrates on practice in all twelve keys – moving higher by half-step – to help develop dexterity and range. The companion CD includes all of the exercises in 12 keys.
00315341 Book/CD Pack..$17.95

Prices, contents & availability
subject to change without notice.

0419
068